Keynote 3

Paul Dummett
Helen Stephenson
Lewis Lansford
and Richard Walker

Australia • Brazil • Mexico • Singapore • United Kingdom • United States

Keynote 3
Paul Dummett, Helen Stephenson, Lewis Lansford, and Richard Walker

Publisher: Andrew Robinson

Executive Editor: Sean Bermingham

Senior Development Editor: Derek Mackrell

Associate Development Editors: Melissa Pang, Yvonne Tan

Director of Global Marketing: Ian Martin

Senior Product Marketing Manager: Caitlin Thomas

IP Analyst: Kyle Cooper

IP Project Manager: Carissa Poweleit

Media Researcher: Leila Hishmeh

Senior Director of Production: Michael Burggren

Senior Content Project Manager: Tan Jin Hock

Manufacturing Planner: Mary Beth Hennebury

Compositor: MPS North America LLC

Cover/Text Design: Brenda Carmichael

Cover Photo: Cyclists reflected in Main-Danube Canal near Nurnberg: © Gerd Ludwig/ National Geographic Creative

© 2017 National Geographic Learning, a part of Cengage Learning

ALL RIGHTS RESERVED. No part of this work covered by the copyright herein may be reproduced or distributed in any form or by any means, except as permitted by U.S. copyright law, without the prior written permission of the copyright owner.

"National Geographic," "National Geographic Society" and the Yellow Border Design are registered trademarks of the National Geographic Society ® Marcas Registradas

> For product information and technology assistance, contact us at
> **Cengage Learning Customer & Sales Support, 1-800-354-9706**
> For permission to use material from this text or product, submit all requests online at **cengage.com/permissions**
> Further permissions questions can be emailed to
> **permissionrequest@cengage.com**

Student Book with My Keynote Online:
ISBN-13: 978-1-337-10412-8

Student Book:
ISBN-13: 978-1-305-96505-8

National Geographic Learning
20 Channel Center Street
Boston, MA 02210
USA

Cengage Learning is a leading provider of customized learning solutions with office locations around the globe, including Singapore, the United Kingdom, Australia, Mexico, Brazil, and Japan. Locate your local office at
international.cengage.com/region

Cengage Learning products are represented in Canada by Nelson Education, Ltd.

Visit National Geographic Learning online at **NGL.cengage.com**
Visit our corporate website at **www.cengage.com**

Printed in China
Print Number: 04   Print Year: 2017

Contents

	Scope and Sequence	6
	Welcome to Keynote!	10
1	Making a Difference	13
2	Trends	25
3	Improving Lives	37
	Presentation 1	49
4	Designing the Web	51
5	Community Builders	63
6	Clear Communication	75
	Presentation 2	87
7	Identity	89
8	Transportation Solutions	101
9	New Words	113
	Presentation 3	125
10	Understanding Emotions	127
11	Leaders and Thinkers	139
12	Well-being	151
	Presentation 4	163
	Communication Activities	165
	TED Talk Transcripts	172
	Grammar Summary	182
	Acknowledgements	191
	Credits	192

Featured TEDTALKS

Mark Bezos

1 A life lesson from a volunteer firefighter

Derek Sivers

2 How to start a movement

Kenneth Shinozuka

3 My simple invention, designed to keep my grandfather safe

Margaret Gould Stewart

4 How giant websites design for you (and a billion others, too)

Haas and Hahn

5 How painting can transform communities

Melissa Marshall

6 Talk nerdy to me

Pico Iyer
7 Where is home?

Sanjay Dastoor
8 A skateboard, with a boost

Anne Curzan
9 What makes a word "real"?

Rana el Kaliouby
10 This app knows how you feel

Richard Branson
11 Life at 30,000 feet

Arianna Huffington
12 How to succeed? Get more sleep

Scope and Sequence

UNIT	LESSON A		LESSON B	
	VOCABULARY	LISTENING	LANGUAGE FOCUS	SPEAKING
1 Making a Difference	Collocations to describe giving help	**Inspiring dreams** *Peter Draw, artist*	**Function** Talking about present and past actions **Grammar** Review of present and past tenses	Talking about ways to help
2 Trends	Collocations to describe trends	**Analyzing trends** *Tara Hirebet, trend expert*	**Function** Talking about future trends **Grammar** Review of future tenses: *will* and *going to*	Describing future trends
3 Improving Lives	Healthcare	**My health routine** *Kate Chong, sports enthusiast*	**Function** Talking about cause and effect **Grammar** Conjunctions for cause and effect	Talking about healthcare tech

PRESENTATION 1 Talking about how you can make a difference

4 Designing the Web	Website features	**Designing websites** *Carrie Cousins, web designer*	**Function** Comparing products and services **Grammar** Comparatives and superlatives, *(not) as … as*, *(very) different from …*, *… the same as …*	Making decisions based on user reviews
5 Community Builders	Words for talking about communities	**Creating green spaces** *Martín Andrade, entrepreneur*	**Function** Talking about how places have changed **Grammar** The passive voice	Describing changes in my community
6 Clear Communication	Communication collocations	**Communication styles** *Neil Anderson, teacher trainer*	**Function** Talking about communication preferences **Grammar** Verb patterns with *-ing* and infinitive	Communication methods

PRESENTATION 2 Suggesting a way to improve communication among residents and strengthen the sense of community in your neighborhood

	LESSON C	LESSON D		LESSON E	
	READING	TED TALK	PRESENTATION SKILLS	COMMUNICATE	WRITING
	Food rescue mission	A LIFE LESSON FROM A VOLUNTEER FIREFIGHTER *Mark Bezos*	Helping your audience visualize	People who have made a difference	Writing about someone who has made a difference in your life
	Identifying trends	HOW TO START A MOVEMENT *Derek Sivers*	Commenting on visuals	Consumer trends	Making predictions about a product or service
	The challenge of Alzheimer's	MY SIMPLE INVENTION, DESIGNED TO KEEP MY GRANDFATHER SAFE *Kenneth Shinozuka*	Opening with interesting facts	Innovative healthcare solutions	Writing a letter about a tech solution for a healthcare issue
	Website design on a giant scale	HOW GIANT WEBSITES DESIGN FOR YOU (AND A BILLION OTHERS, TOO) *Margaret Gould Stewart*	Asking the audience questions	Improving user experiences	Writing a review of your cell phone
	Barefoot College	HOW PAINTING CAN TRANSFORM COMMUNITIES *Haas and Hahn*	Ending with a hope for the future	A neighborhood survey	Writing a letter about improving your neighborhood
	Communication in the digital age	TALK NERDY TO ME *Melissa Marshall*	Engaging with your audience	Explaining a topic of interest	Writing what you learned about a topic

Scope and Sequence

UNIT		LESSON A		LESSON B	
		VOCABULARY	LISTENING	LANGUAGE FOCUS	SPEAKING
7	Identity	Words for talking about identity	**Multicultural experiences** *Janice Reis Lodge, manager*	**Function** Talking about ongoing actions and events **Grammar** Present perfect progressive	Talking about living abroad
8	Transportation Solutions	Transportation collocations	**An unusual commute** *Cyril Burguiere, SUP enthusiast*	**Function** Making predictions **Grammar** *will* and *might*	Changes in global travel
9	New Words	Words for talking about language	**Collecting words** *Charles Browne, English professor*	**Function** Talking about changes **Grammar** *used to*	Talking about changes in meaning

PRESENTATION 3 Describing someone you know

10	Understanding Emotions	Feelings	**Dealing with emotions** *Craig Albrightson, guidance counselor*	**Function** Reporting other people's speech and thoughts **Grammar** Reported speech	Talking about EQ in jobs
11	Leaders and Thinkers	Collocations for talking about doing business	**Starting a business** *Priscilla Shunmugam, fashion designer*	**Function** Talking about obligation and giving advice **Grammar** Modals of necessity	Interview with a CEO
12	Well-being	Words for describing health and well-being	**What your brain does when you sleep** *Jeffrey Iliff, neuroscientist*	**Function** Talking about imaginary situations **Grammar** Second conditional	Describing your ideal lifestyle

PRESENTATION 4 Recommending a way to achieve better work-life balance

	LESSON C	LESSON D		LESSON E	
	READING	TED TALK	PRESENTATION SKILLS	COMMUNICATE	WRITING
	Global migration	**WHERE IS HOME?** *Pico Iyer*	Using stories to personalize your message	A survey on identity	Writing about factors that contribute to one's identity
	Unique commutes	**A SKATEBOARD, WITH A BOOST** *Sanjay Dastoor*	Signposting	Inventing a transportation device	Creating a poster of a transportation device
	Language change	**WHAT MAKES A WORD "REAL"?** *Anne Curzan*	Closing the loop	Guessing meanings	Writing about the effect of the Internet on the English language
	Emotion in technology	**THIS APP KNOWS HOW YOU FEEL** *Rana el Kaliouby*	Giving a demonstration	Applications of emotion-sensing technology	Writing about whether there is a need for technology to recognize emotions
	Lessons in business	**LIFE AT 30,000 FEET** *Richard Branson*	Quoting people	My business philosophy	Writing about how you would run a company
	Achieving work-life balance	**HOW TO SUCCEED? GET MORE SLEEP** *Arianna Huffington*	Using humor	Debate on work-life balance	Writing about how you could improve your productivity

Welcome to Keynote!

In this book, you will develop your English language skills and explore great ideas with an authentic TED Talk. Each unit topic is based around a TED speaker's main idea.

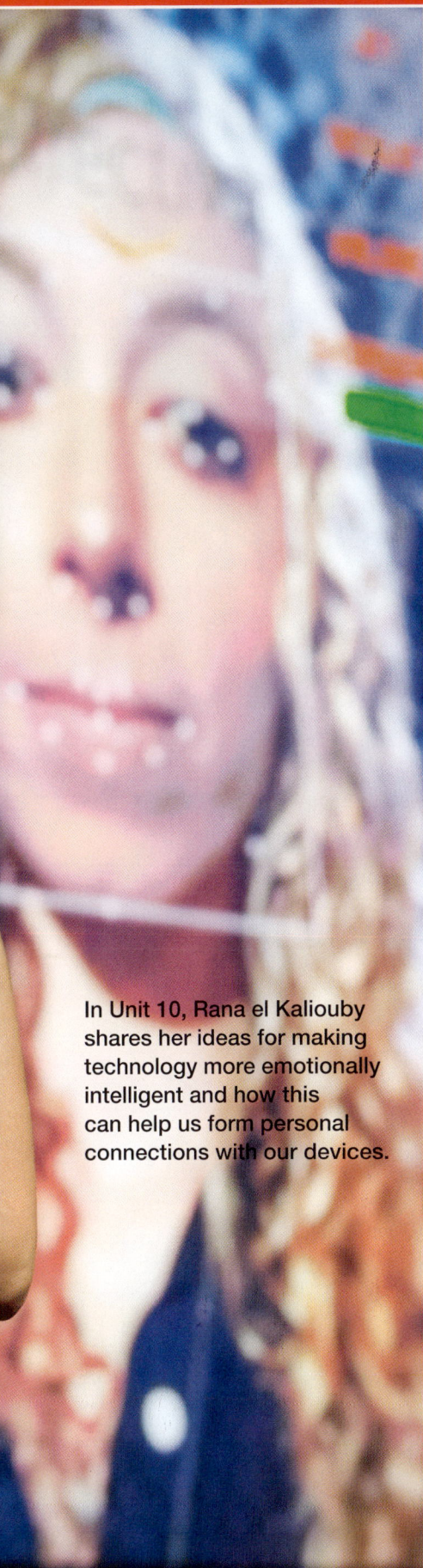

In Unit 10, Rana el Kaliouby shares her ideas for making technology more emotionally intelligent and how this can help us form personal connections with our devices.

LISTENING AND SPEAKING

- Practice listening to real people talking about the unit topic. Real-life people featured in this book include an artist, an entrepreneur, and a guidance counselor.

- Develop your **speaking confidence** with a model conversation and guided speaking tasks.

See pages **129, 131**

VOCABULARY AND GRAMMAR

- In each unit, you'll learn key words, phrases, and grammar structures for talking about the unit topic.

- Build **language and visual literacy skills** with real-life information—in Unit 10, you'll learn about emotional intelligence and the characteristics of people with high EQ.

See pages **128, 130**

READING

- Develop your **reading and vocabulary skills** with a specially adapted reading passage. In Unit 10, you'll learn about the applications and challenges of emotionally intelligent technology.

- The passage includes several words and phrases that appear later in the TED Talk.

See pages **132–134**

VIEWING

- Practice your viewing and **critical thinking** skills as you watch a specially adapted TED Talk.

- Notice how TED speakers use effective language and **communication** skills to present their ideas.

See pages **135–137**

COMMUNICATING AND PRESENTING

- Use your **creativity** and **collaboration skills** in a final task that reviews language and ideas from the unit.

See page **138**

- Build your **speaking confidence** further in a Presentation task (after every three units).

See page **163**

WRITING

- Communicate your own ideas about the unit topic in a controlled writing task.

See page **138**

- Develop your **writing and language skills** further in the **Keynote Workbook** and online at **MyKeynoteOnline**.

What is TED?

TED has a simple goal: to spread great ideas. Every year, hundreds of presenters share ideas at TED events around the world. Millions of people watch TED Talks online. The talks inspire many people to change their attitudes and their lives.

SPREADING IDEAS WORLDWIDE

Over 10,000 TEDx events in 167 countries

Over 2,200 TEDTALKS recorded

TEDTALKS translated into 105 languages

Over 1,000,000,000 views of TEDTALKS at TED.com

1 Making a Difference

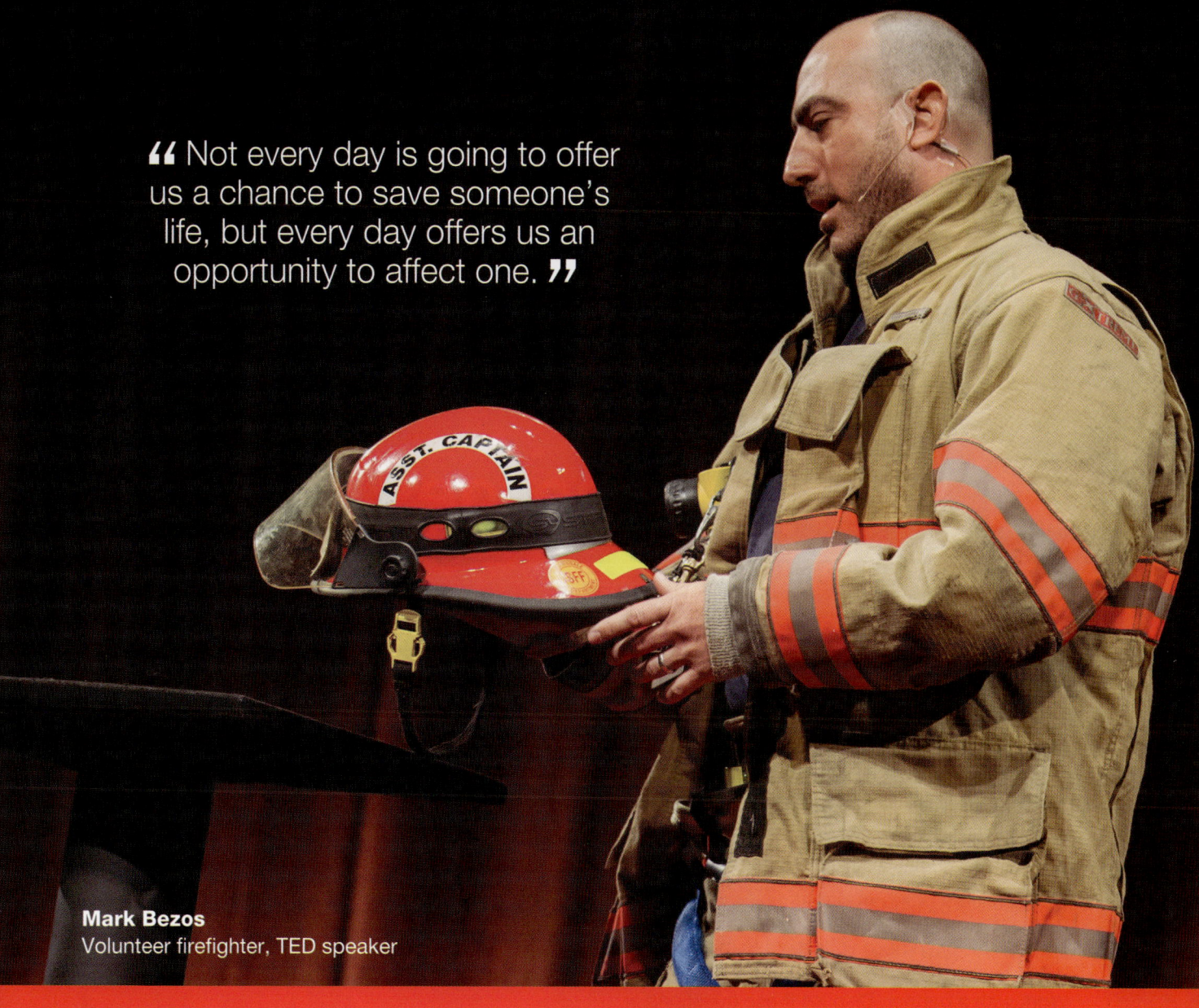

" Not every day is going to offer us a chance to save someone's life, but every day offers us an opportunity to affect one. "

Mark Bezos
Volunteer firefighter, TED speaker

UNIT GOALS

In this unit, you will …

- talk about how people can make a difference.
- read about how simple actions can help others.
- watch a TED Talk about a life lesson from a volunteer firefighter.

WARM UP

▶ **1.1** Watch part of Mark Bezos's TED Talk. Answer the questions with a partner.

1 What situation is Bezos describing? What was he asked to do?

2 Look through the unit. What are some ways we can help people?

Volunteers unloading food supplies in Yogyakarta, Indonesia

1A Everyday heroes

VOCABULARY Giving help

A ▶ **1.2** Complete the sentences. Circle the most suitable words. Then listen and check your answers.

1 Even small acts of kindness can (**take care of** / **make a difference to**) people's lives.

2 When friends go through difficult times, it's important to (**be there for** / **make an impact on**) them.

3 The work of great people, like Nelson Mandela, (**helps out** / **makes an impact on**) millions of people's lives.

4 Doctors and nurses (**inspire** / **take care of**) sick and injured people.

5 Scientists can (**be there for** / **inspire**) positive changes in the world through their work.

6 Charities often need volunteers to (**help out at** / **inspire**) their events.

B Work with a partner. Discuss these questions.

1 What are some jobs or professions in which people help others? What do they involve? Would you like to do any of them?

2 When was the last time you helped take care of someone? What did you do?

3 Is there someone who inspires or has inspired you?

> One job in which people help others is …

> I would be interested in being a(n) … because …

LISTENING Inspiring dreams

> **Expressing beliefs and wishes**
>
> Here are some common expressions we can use to talk about our wishes.
>
> I hope to …   I want to …   It's my dream to …

A ▶ **1.3** Watch artist Peter Draw talk about his work. What are some of the ways he affects people's lives?

☐ He teaches art to children.
☐ He designs homes for people.
☐ He raises money for sick children.
☐ He uses art to help disaster survivors.

B ▶ **1.3** Watch again. Complete the information about the lessons Peter Draw has learned.

1 It's important to work hard and _____.

2 Every little thing we do can _____.

3 Don't wait to _____.

Peter Draw with a student in Fukushima, Japan

C CRITICAL THINKING

Reflecting How does Peter Draw feel his work is helping to make a difference in the world?

SPEAKING Talking about helping people

A ▶ **1.4** What did Speaker B help with?

A: Do people often ask you for help?
B: Yeah, sometimes. People usually ask me to repair things, because I'm good at it.
A: So have you helped anyone recently?
B: Yeah, my brother. He needed help with his bicycle because the wheel was damaged.
A: When was that?
B: It was last month.
A: And how did it go?
B: I replaced the wheel for him, and he was really happy!

B Practice the conversation with a partner.

C Work with a partner. Talk about some ways you have helped other people. Use the expressions in blue above to help you.

> People usually ask me to help them move house because I have a big van.

> Have you helped anyone move recently?

1B Making an impact

LANGUAGE FOCUS Discussing ways to contribute

A ▶ **1.5** Read the information. Give some examples of how you can do these things.

10 WAYS YOU CAN **MAKE A DIFFERENCE**

Sometimes, small actions can have a big impact on someone else's life. Here are some ways we can help people around us.

1. Listen to someone
2. Run an errand for a busy friend
3. Cook a meal for someone
4. Teach a skill
5. Donate things you don't need
6. Show appreciation
7. Accompany someone on a walk
8. Volunteer your time
9. Share inspiring stories
10. Recycle

B ▶ **1.6** Listen to the conversation. What did the woman at the grocery store do to help the elderly couple?

C ▶ **1.7** Watch and study the language in the chart.

Talking about present and past actions
Peter Draw **uses** art to make a difference in people's lives. I**'m making** dolls to sell at a charity fair. Many scientists **are working** to make the world a better place.
The volunteers **cleaned up** the beach. I helped an injured cat when I **was volunteering** at an animal shelter. The nurses **were talking** to my grandfather when I visited him at the hospital.
The Internet **has changed** the way we help people in need. Governments around the world **have signed** an agreement to fight climate change.

For more information on **present and past tenses**, see Grammar Summary 1 on pages 182–183.

D ▶ **1.6** Listen to the conversation in **B** again. Complete the sentences from the conversation.

1. "I _____ in line, and there _____ a few people in front of me."

2. "An elderly couple _____ at the front of the line."

3. "The elderly couple _____ pretty surprised at first, and _____ to take her money."

E Complete the sentences. Circle the correct words.

1. It (**became** / **has become**) really easy to raise money for a good cause online. It (**took** / **is taking**) me just a few minutes to learn how to use a fundraising website yesterday.

2. Whenever I (**went** / **go**) to the recycling center, I see lots of people who (**are recycling** / **were recycling**) their trash.

3. A few weeks ago, I (**am teaching** / **taught**) my grandmother how to make video calls.

4. People (**are beginning** / **begin**) to show more concern for the environment.

5. (**Have you ever done** / **Were you doing**) volunteer work for a charity? I (**do** / **did**) last year, and I (**thought** / **have thought**) it was a great experience.

F ▶ **1.8** Complete the information using the correct form of the words in parentheses. Then listen and check your answers.

There ¹_____ (**be**) lots of small things we can do to make a difference in people's lives. In 2010, 12-year-old Blare Gooch ²_____ (**watch**) TV when he ³_____ (**see**) a news program about the Haiti earthquake. On it, a young boy was crying. Blare ⁴_____ (**can't**) stop thinking about what he had seen, and wanted to help in some way. He thought of an idea to collect teddy bears for the children in Haiti. He ⁵_____ (**start**) a project called Blare's Bears for Haiti. Through Facebook, he got many schools to ⁶_____ (**donate**) bears. Blare managed to collect 25,000 bears for Haiti. "It doesn't really matter how small or old you are," he says. "If you're young and think you can't make a big difference in the world, well, you actually can."

Blare Gooch with all the bears he has collected

SPEAKING Talking about ways to help

Work with a partner. Look at the infographic on page 16. Then discuss these questions.

1. Which ideas would you like to try? Why?
2. Which ideas do you think are the most helpful?
3. Can you think of other ideas to add to the list?

> I want to recycle trash. It's important for everyone to help make our environment better.

> I think showing more appreciation to people around you can make a big difference in people's lives.

1C Food rescue mission

PRE-READING Skimming

Skim the article. How does Robert Lee help make a difference in his city?

▶ 1.9

1   When you hear the word *hero*, you may think of someone like Mahatma Gandhi, who **devoted** his life working for his country's independence. But there are also
5   many "everyday" heroes—they may not create change on a global scale, but they do what they can to help make a difference in people's lives. Everyday heroes are normal people who are **passionate** about making the world a better
10 place. One such person is Robert Lee.

   Lee grew up in New York City. As his family was not rich, he learned from a young age the importance of **minimizing** food wastage. When he was in college, he was part of a student group
15 that delivered leftover food to homeless shelters. This experience made him realize how serious the problem of food wastage actually was.

   After graduating from New York University, Lee and a college friend created a nonprofit[1]
20 organization called Rescuing Leftover Cuisine. Its purpose is to collect unsold food from restaurants and deliver it to homeless shelters and food kitchens. Volunteers pick up food from restaurants around the city and distribute it to those in need.
25 The process is simple. Using an app developed by Lee and his team, restaurants report the amount of leftover food that they have each day, and then volunteers sign up for delivery slots. The delivery routes are usually short, so volunteers can deliver
30 the food they've collected simply by walking from the restaurants to the shelters. Lee believes this is a very efficient method of delivery.

   To date, Lee and his team have successfully rescued over 150,000 kilograms of food, serving
35 almost 300,000 meals to people who need them. Lee has shown how we can take small actions to improve the lives of people around us. A simple idea or action may sometimes seem **insignificant**, but it may have an impact greater
40 than you can imagine. But Lee says that his work isn't over: "It's just the beginning. The need is so great, and there's just so much demand. With more restaurants, who knows how much more we can do."

[1] **nonprofit:** *adj.* not working with the aim of making money

Robert Lee and a group of volunteers collecting food

A third or more of all food produced in the world is lost or wasted—over **one billion tons** every year.

This amount of food waste is more than enough to feed the estimated **900 million** people in the world who don't have enough food.

In the United States, about **40 percent** of food goes to waste, while **one-sixth** of the population can't afford to have regular meals.

UNDERSTANDING MAIN IDEAS

What is the main purpose of the passage?

    a to explain how Robert Lee got the idea for his organization

    b to show an example of how regular people can make a difference

    c to explore the problem of food waste in restaurants and households

UNDERSTANDING A SEQUENCE

How does Rescuing Leftover Cuisine work? Order the stages from 1 to 6.

_____ A volunteer agrees to take on the delivery job.

_____ A restaurant is given an app that Lee's team developed.

_____ People in need receive food from the volunteer.

_____ The restaurant reports how much food it has left at the end of the day.

_____ The volunteer picks up unsold food from the restaurant.

_____ The volunteer walks to a homeless shelter with the leftover food.

BUILDING VOCABULARY

A Match the words in blue from the passage to their definitions.

    1 devoted   ○   ○ unimportant

    2 passionate   ○   ○ reducing

    3 minimizing   ○   ○ having strong feelings or beliefs

    4 insignificant   ○   ○ gave all or most of one's effort or time

B Complete the sentences with the correct form of the words in **A**.

    1 Many researchers have _____ their lives to finding a cure for cancer.

    2 Countries need to work together in order to _____ the impact of climate change.

    3 People who are _____ about their jobs tend to work hard and do well.

    4 We should all do what we can to help others. No contribution is _____.

C CRITICAL THINKING

Reflecting Work with a partner. Look at the infographic on page 19. How do you think so much food gets wasted?

> Food sometimes gets wasted when we …

> Sometimes at the supermarket …

1D A life lesson from a volunteer firefighter

TEDTALKS

MARK BEZOS works for a charity organization, Robin Hood, which fights **poverty** in New York City. He's also a **volunteer** firefighter in Westchester County, New York, where he lives. Mark Bezos is continuously amazed and motivated by the **acts** of heroism—big and small—that he sees every day.

Mark Bezos's idea worth spreading is that every act of **generosity** matters—even the small ones.

PREVIEWING

Read the paragraphs above. Match each **bold** word to its meaning. You will hear these words in the TED Talk.

1 the state of being extremely poor   _____
2 the quality of being kind and helpful   _____
3 someone who does a job for no pay   _____
4 things done or achieved   _____

VIEWING

A ▶ **1.10** Watch Part 1 of the TED Talk. Choose the correct options.

1 In Bezos's town, there's _____.
   a a lack of skilled firefighters
   b a lack of volunteer firefighters
   c a team of professional firefighters

2 Which word best describes how Mark Bezos felt about his first fire?
   a excited   b nervous   c worried

3 The woman was probably _____ when the fire started.
   a sleeping   b cooking   c taking a bath

B ▶ **1.11** Watch Part 2 of the TED Talk. Put the events in the order they happened.

   a Bezos carried the shoes downstairs and gave them to the homeowner.
   b The homeowner sent a letter thanking the firefighters.
   c The captain asked Bezos to go into the house and bring back some shoes.
   d The captain asked the other volunteer to rescue a dog from inside the house.

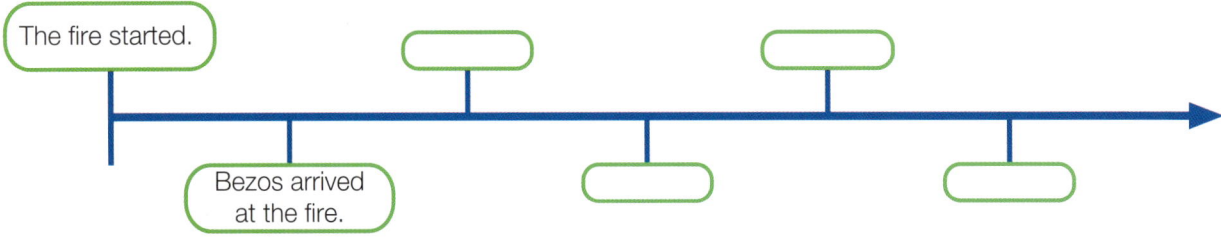

C ▶ **1.12** Watch Part 3 of the TED Talk. Discuss these questions with a partner.

   1 What has Mark Bezos learned from the acts of kindness, courage, or generosity that he has seen?
   2 Mark Bezos's message to his audience is "Don't wait." What does he mean by this?

D **CRITICAL THINKING**

   Inferring Work with a partner. Why do you think Bezos refers to the other firefighter as Lex Luthor (Superman's enemy)? How do you think he really feels about the other volunteer?

Robin Hood volunteer Jasmine Wood reading to a group of children who live in a shelter in New York

VOCABULARY IN CONTEXT

A ▶ **1.13** Watch the excerpts from the TED Talk. Choose the correct meaning of the words.

B Complete the sentences using the words in the box.

| witness to | get in on | assignments | above all |

1 To _____ the online discussion, you can visit the Facebook page.

2 As a volunteer, I'm often _____ how people's lives can be improved through our help.

3 Employees should be hardworking and skilled in their jobs, but _____ they should be team players.

4 Working on group _____ helps people learn teamwork.

PRESENTATION SKILLS Helping your audience visualize

> To make your presentation more memorable, help your audience visualize the points you are making. You can do this by:
> - giving a demonstration
> - telling a story
> - using pictures and visuals
> - sharing interesting facts or statistics

A ▶ **1.14** Watch part of Mark Bezos's TED Talk. What methods does he use to help his audience visualize?

B ▶ **1.14** Watch again. Complete the sentences.

1 "… she was standing outside in the _____ rain, under an _____ , in her pajamas, _____ , while her house was in flames."

2 "… off I went—up the _____ , _____ the hall, _____ the 'real' firefighters …"

C Work with a partner. What methods would you use to help your audience visualize the following?

1 the problem of food wastage around the world
2 a group of people in our society who need care but are often overlooked
3 how someone has helped make a difference in other people's lives
4 how recycling trash is good for the environment

> I'd share facts and data about the amount of food we waste.

23

1E Touching lives

COMMUNICATE People who have made a difference

A Think of someone you know who has made a difference in your life. It could be someone you know personally—a friend, relative, or teacher—or someone you have read or heard about.

B Write some notes about your experience with the person. Use the questions to help you.

- What has that person done to make an impact on you?
- When was it?
- What changes did it make in your life?
- How did the experience make you feel?
- How did it change your thoughts or actions?

C Work with a partner. Talk about how that person has made a difference in your life.

> **Describing how people have made an impact**
> I was inspired to …   He motivated me to …
> It transformed the way I … He changed my mind about …

> Someone who has made an impact on my life is …

> One thing that he did that really made a difference is …

> What she did made me realize that …

WRITING Describing a personal experience

Write a paragraph about the person who has made an impact on your life and what you gained from that experience.

> Someone who has made a big difference in my life is my teacher. She showed me that …

Students attending class on a "boat school" in Bangladesh

2 Trends

"If you really care about starting a movement, have the courage to follow and show others how to follow."

Derek Sivers
Author, TED speaker

UNIT GOALS

In this unit, you will ...

- talk about consumer and technological trends.
- read about how to identify trends.
- watch a TED Talk about how to start a movement.

WARM UP

▶ 2.1 Watch part of Derek Sivers's TED Talk. Answer the questions with a partner.

1 What is happening in the video Sivers shows? What do you think he is going to talk about?

2 Look through the unit. What examples of trends or movements can you find?

From business trends to the latest fashion, trends can be found all around us.

2A Trends around us

VOCABULARY Describing trends

A ▶ 2.2 Circle the correct words. Then listen and check your answers.

1 The economy is doing very well. It is (**growing** / **shrinking**) fast.

2 The number of young people who smoke is (**increasing** / **decreasing**) because of greater health awareness.

3 I eat out more often these days as the quality of food in many restaurants has (**improved** / **gotten worse**).

4 Unhealthy food choices such as fast food are causing health problems like obesity to become (**less common** / **more widespread**).

5 In 1980, the average age of a person in the United States was 30. Now, it has (**risen** / **fallen**) to nearly 40.

6 The Internet has become a part of people's lives. (**Fewer and fewer** / **More and more**) people are shopping or watching TV programs online.

7 Between 1970 and 2014, more affluent households got even (**poorer** / **richer**); their average earnings increased by 47%.

B Complete the sentences describing trends. Use your own ideas.

1 The number of people who _____ has decreased in the last few years.

2 _____ has improved over time.

3 _____ is/are becoming less common nowadays.

4 These days, fewer and fewer people _____ .

5 _____ is/are getting richer.

6 The problem of _____ has become more widespread in the last five years.

C Work with a partner. Do you agree with your partner's statements in **B**? Why or why not?

> I agree that the number of people who …

LISTENING Analyzing trends

> **Summarizing details**
> To check your understanding of what someone said, you can respond with a summary of his or her ideas.
> So you mean …?   So what you're saying is …?

A ▶ **2.3** Watch trend expert Tara Hirebet talk about the work she does. Check (✓) the things that her job involves.

☐ reading magazines, articles, books, and blogs
☐ developing advertisements for companies
☐ spending time with consumers
☐ designing logos for businesses

Tara Hirebet is an expert on consumer trends in Asia.

B ▶ **2.4** Watch the next part of the interview and complete the sentences.

1 Trend spotting helps companies learn about their competitors, _____ preferences, and new forms of _____.
2 Hirebet has done trend spotting for _____, technology departments, and startups.
3 Hirebet helped an international sports brand succeed in the _____ youth market.

C CRITICAL THINKING

Evaluating In which industries is it most important to spot trends? Why?

SPEAKING Talking about trends

A ▶ **2.5** Does Speaker A like music streaming?

A: I just signed up for an account on a music-streaming website.
B: Yeah? Streaming music has become really popular in the last few years. So how do you like it so far?
A: I love it. Especially how easy it is to search for different kinds of music. And the best part is it also gives me good recommendations for other artists to listen to.
B: I know. It's completely changed the way people listen to music.
A: Yeah. It's so much more convenient this way. Anyway, I don't have a lot of space in my apartment to keep CDs.

B Practice the conversation with a partner.

C Work with a partner. What are some trends you have adopted recently? What do you think of them? Use the expressions in blue above to help you.

> I just started getting into online shopping.

> Really? How do you like it so far?

2B Trends in technology

LANGUAGE FOCUS Discussing future trends

A ▶ **2.6** Read the timeline. Give some examples of smart devices that you use.

THE INTERNET OF THINGS

The Internet of Things is made up of billions of smart devices that use wireless technology to send information to one another and to us.

1991 Birth of the World Wide Web connects computers.

2006 **Two billion** devices are connected to the Internet.

2008 More things connected to the Internet than there are people.

2012 **10%** of cars are connected to the Internet.

2020 **90%** of cars will be connected to the Internet. There will be **200 billion** Internet-connected things: around **26** smart objects for every human on Earth.

THE FUTURE ▶▶▶ Robots may be able to learn from one another and work in teams to solve problems. There may be a "Facebook of things"—a platform for smart devices.

B ▶ **2.7** Listen to the conversation. What kind of device does the man want?

The man wants a(n) _____.

C ▶ **2.8** Watch and study the language in the chart.

Talking about future trends

I don't think there **will be** flying cars anytime soon.
Smart devices in the home **will become** very popular over the next few years.
In twenty years, there **won't be** many people without smartphones.

Streaming music **is going to become** the most popular way of listening to music.
Most home appliances **are going to be** connected to the Internet within five years.
Robots are becoming more common, but they **aren't going to replace** humans in all professions.

For more information on **will** and **going to**, see Grammar Summary 2 on page 183.

D ▶ 2.7 Listen to the conversation in B again. How is the device going to help the man achieve his goal? Complete the sentences from the conversation.

1 "I think _____ lose weight."

2 "_____ monitor how much fat I'm losing."

3 "I think _____ for seeing what types of exercises are better for achieving my goals."

4 "I can record the date that I started doing yoga, and _____ track how well it's helping me lose weight."

E ▶ 2.9 Complete the information. Circle the correct words. Then listen and check your answers.

In the twenty-first century, we ¹(**have already seen** / **will see**) three tech revolutions: the rise of broadband, mobile, and the birth of social media. Experts ²(**predict** / **will predict**) that over the next five to ten years, the next tech revolution ³(**connects** / **is going to connect**) billions of devices to the Internet. This is called the Internet of Things—an entire network of devices that are able to "talk" to one another. With this technology, we ⁴(**will be able to create** / **were creating**) "smart" devices that we can use in our everyday lives. Daniel Burrus, a technology forecaster, believes that there are going to be many new and interesting ways we can use this technology. The Internet of Things ⁵(**changed** / **is going to change**) the way we work, play, and sleep. Life ⁶(**will be** / **is**) very different by 2025.

A "smart" home system allows users to control electronic devices in their homes.

F Complete the sentences with your own ideas.

1 Within the next few years, there will be _____.

2 I think _____ is/are going to become popular in the next five years.

3 By 2030, there will probably be _____.

SPEAKING Describing future trends

Work with a partner. Take turns describing and explaining your ideas in **F** above.

> I think within the next few years, there will be more "smart" vehicles on the road.

> Yeah, I think so, too. Within the next few years, maybe we'll also see other "smart" objects, such as waste bins that can automatically separate trash into different types!

2C Identifying trends

PRE-READING Skimming

Skim the article. Check (✓) the topics that the passage mentions.

- ☐ characteristics of trends
- ☐ trend-spotting tools
- ☐ jobs in trend spotting
- ☐ upcoming business trends

▶ 2.10

1 Businesses need to predict change and spot **emerging** trends in order to stay **relevant** and beat the competition. But how can they know what the next big thing is before everyone else?

FADS VERSUS TRENDS

2 One important step in identifying trends is to distinguish[1] them from fads, which don't last long. In 2011, a craze called "planking"—where people photographed themselves lying face down, usually in an odd public place—became popular. However, this turned out to be nothing more than a fad.

3 It's often hard to tell the difference between trends and fads in the early stages. But there are several signs we can look out for. First, trends can make money; businesses should be able to see how they can **take advantage of** a new trend and plan long-term strategies. Second, trends tend to link with one another. For example, the trend of online shopping is related to a bigger trend—the rise of electronic commerce.[2] And third, trends usually appeal[3] to a wide range of people. Planking fails in all three areas, and sure enough, by early 2012, it started to lose popularity.

4 Another way of spotting trends is to observe people's hobbies. The idea for social networking sites like Facebook, Instagram, and Snapchat came from noticing that people like to share photographs or personal information in their free time.

IN SEARCH OF TRENDS

5 The importance of spotting trends has led to a growing industry with a range of new jobs. These vary from individual trend consultants to entire teams of people in large corporations. Social media analysts—a job title that didn't even exist before the mid-2000s—look through huge amounts of data online. Kevin Allocca, whose job is to **analyze** trends on YouTube, spends his day monitoring news headlines and popular videos to help his company look out for industry trends.

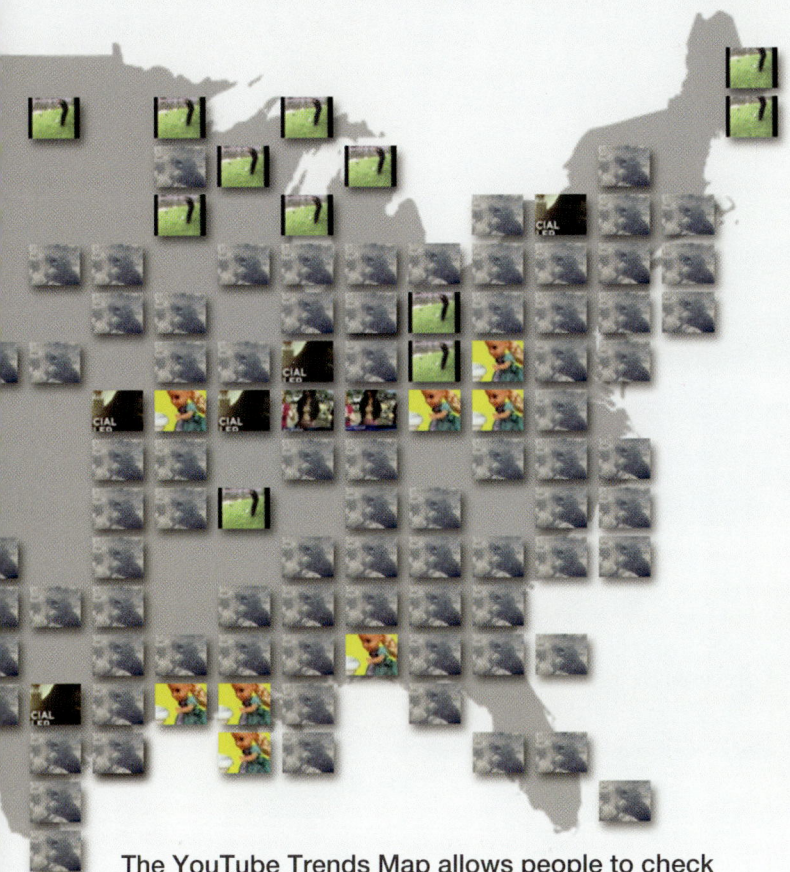
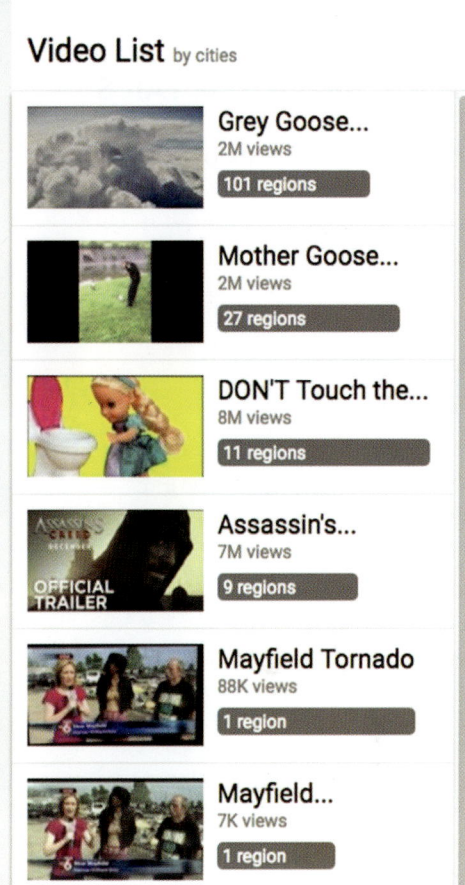

The YouTube Trends Map allows people to check out the most popular videos in their area.

NEW TECHNOLOGY

6 New forms of technology also aid trend spotters. Allocca uses organization tools such as gReader Pro and NetNewsWire to help filter[4] the many websites he monitors every day.

7 Predictive tech analyzes online conversations, blogs, videos, and even photo descriptions. Predictive tech apps search the Web for keywords such as *trend*, *becoming more*, and *recently*, and then compares the data to find common topics.

8 There are also predictive tech websites that encourage trend spotters to work together and submit ideas for new trends. Springwise is a website that allows its members to submit business ideas that they think will work in their city or country. If a member's idea is featured on the website, they receive points that can be exchanged for money.

9 Trend spotting isn't easy, but it is an important skill. Businesses around the world are competing to find the next big thing, and only those that are able to predict and make use of trends will come out on top.

---

[1] **distinguish:** *v.* to notice a difference between people or things
[2] **commerce:** *n.* the buying and selling of goods and services
[3] **appeal:** *v.* to be liked by people
[4] **filter:** *v.* to separate and remove unwanted materials

UNDERSTANDING MAIN IDEAS

Match each section of the passage to its purpose.

1 Paragraphs 2–4 ○   ○ to show how technology can help in predicting trends

2 Paragraph 5 ○   ○ to highlight the characteristics of trends

3 Paragraphs 6–8 ○   ○ to describe jobs in trend spotting

UNDERSTANDING DETAILS

Complete the concept map.

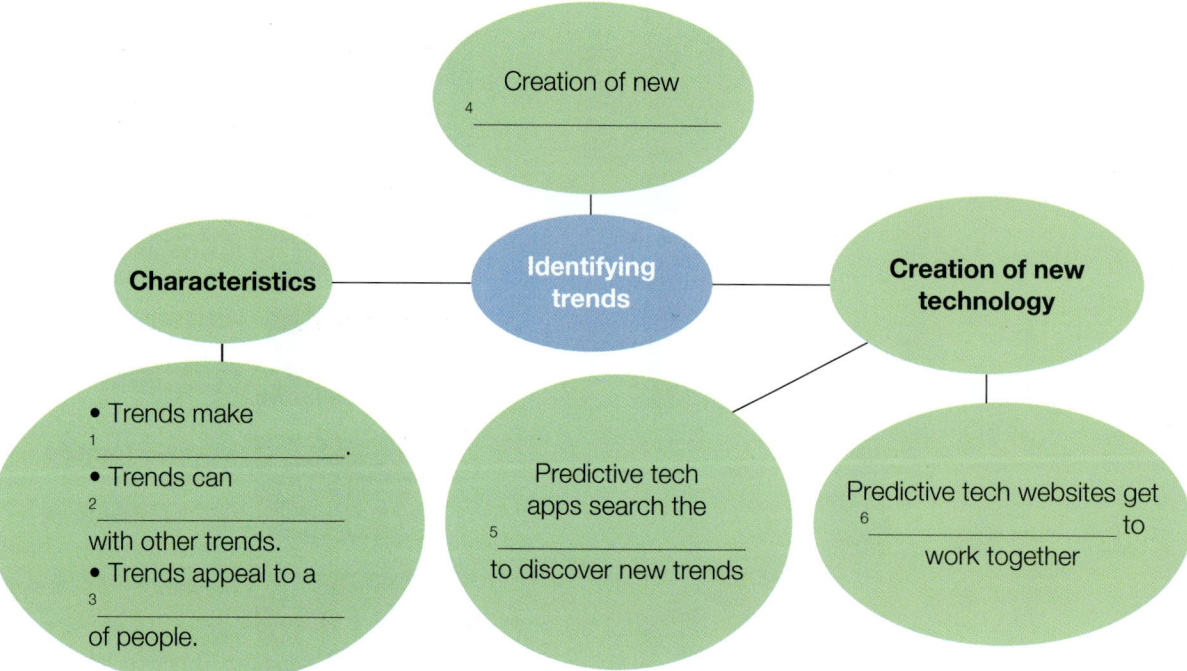

BUILDING VOCABULARY

A Match the words in blue from the passage to their definitions.

1 emerging ○   ○ growing, upcoming

2 relevant ○   ○ study

3 take advantage of ○   ○ appropriate

4 analyze ○   ○ make use of

B CRITICAL THINKING

Inferring Work with a partner. Which statement below do you think the author would agree with? Why?

1 Jobs like social media analyst show how important trend spotting has become.

2 Predictive technologies have begun to replace human trend spotters.

2D How to start a movement

TEDTALKS

DEREK SIVERS is best known as the founder of CD Baby, one of the first sellers of independent music on the Internet. His company, Wood Egg, advises people on how to build companies.

Derek Sivers's idea worth spreading is that while leaders get the credit for starting a movement, the first followers are often the driving force.

PREVIEWING

Read the sentences. Choose the option that has a similar meaning to each **bold** word. You will hear these words in the TED Talk.

1 You need **guts** to stand up and share your ideas with thousands of people.

   a courage   b ability

2 With the speed of change today, having skilled and resourceful workers is **crucial** to many companies' success.

   a useful   b extremely important

3 Successful business ideas are those that are creative and that **stand out**.

   a are practical   b are noticeable in a crowd

4 A movement often begins with just one **lone** voice.

   a single   b clear

5 When Darwin proposed his theory of evolution, he was **ridiculed** by many people.

   a laughed at   b respected

VIEWING

A ▶ **2.11** Watch Part 1 of the TED Talk. Choose the most suitable options.

1 What is the job of the first follower?

   a to have the courage to stand out
   b to show others how to follow

2 What do you think will happen when the first follower joins?

   a Other people will want to join in.
   b People will ignore him and the leader.

33

B ▶ **2.12** Watch Part 2 of the TED Talk. Match the descriptions to the pictures showing the stages of the movement.

a A few more people join.

b People rush to join in so that they can be part of the in-crowd.

c A second follower joins.

d People start to join the group at a faster rate, creating momentum. This is the tipping point.

C ▶ **2.13** Watch Part 3 of the TED Talk. Circle the correct words to complete the advice Sivers gives.

1 The most important thing for a leader to do is to (**have a good idea** / **treat the first followers as equals**).

2 People should not be afraid of (**being the first follower** / **starting their own movement**) when they see someone doing something great.

D CRITICAL THINKING

Inferring Work with a partner. Do you think that people sometimes join a movement or trend because they are afraid of not being part of the in-crowd? Can you think of some examples?

VOCABULARY IN CONTEXT

A ▶ **2.14** Watch the excerpts from the TED Talk. Choose the correct meaning of the words.

B Complete the sentences using the words in the box.

emulate	sit on the fence	nurture	over-glorified

1 People usually _____ people who inspire them.

2 Schools have a duty to _____ the talents of all their students.

3 When you need to decide who to vote into government, you can't _____.

4 Sivers feels that leadership is _____ because no one becomes a leader without someone else's support.

PRESENTATION SKILLS Commenting on visuals

> As you show your visuals, draw the audience's attention to them and highlight the important parts.

A ▶ **2.15** Watch part of Derek Sivers's TED Talk. Check (✓) the expressions he uses in his talk to comment on the visuals.

☐ So here's …
☐ Now, notice that …
☐ Can you see …?
☐ Now, there he is …
☐ So, pay attention to …
☐ So, over the next minute, you'll see …

B Work with a partner. Brainstorm more phrases you could use to draw attention to visuals in a presentation.

C Work with a partner. Choose a video and take turns commenting on the key parts of your video.

> If you look at the man on the right, you'll see that he's taking a photo of himself. Notice that …

2E Predicting trends

COMMUNICATE Consumer trends

A You are going to read about some innovations. **Student A:** Turn to page 165.
Student B: Turn to page 166.

B Work with a partner. Take turns explaining what the innovations are.

> This is a type of technology that allows people to …

> With this product, people can now …

C Discuss with a partner. Which of these innovations you read or heard about do you think will become more popular in the future? Use the following questions to help you.

Who will the product or service be good for?

What possible applications could there be, and how will people benefit from it?

What other trends would it support?

Describing probability
It's likely to …   It will probably …
I think we'll see …   There's a possibility that …

WRITING Making a prediction

Write a description of the product or service you read about and your predictions about it.

> Mobile payment technology will probably become a bigger trend in the future. Smartphones have become very common, so people may …

Some smartphones allow users to pay using their mobile phones.

3 Improving Lives

" I really believe that sensors can improve the quality of life of the elderly. "

Kenneth Shinozuka
Inventor, TED speaker

UNIT GOALS

In this unit, you will ...

- talk about healthcare issues and solutions.
- read about the challenges of an aging population.
- watch a TED Talk about how technology can make life better for patients and their caregivers.

WARM UP

▶ **3.1** Watch part of Kenneth Shinozuka's TED Talk. Answer the questions with a partner.

1 What healthcare issue does Shinozuka identify as most serious in the United States?

2 What do you know about this healthcare issue?

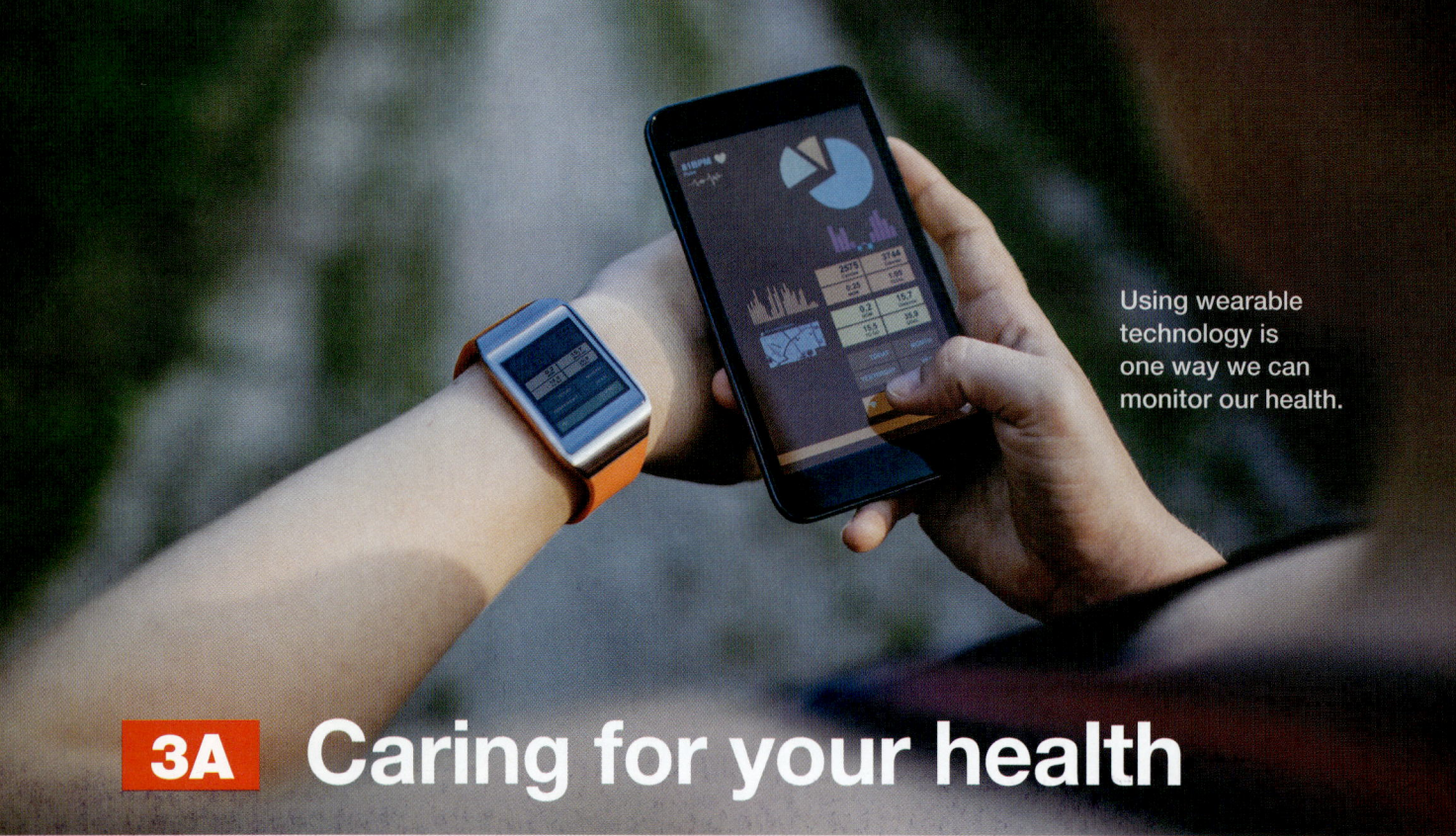

Using wearable technology is one way we can monitor our health.

3A Caring for your health

VOCABULARY Talking about healthcare

A ▶ **3.2** Complete the information using the words in the box. Two words are extra. Then listen and check your answers.

| treatments | caregiver | elderly | suffer from |
| cure | monitor | wearable | motivate |

As populations grow older and the number of [1]_____ people rises, healthcare is becoming increasingly expensive and complicated. Elderly people naturally [2]_____ more health problems and may need a variety of [3]_____. One solution is [4]_____ technology—small, light devices that people can carry with them. By measuring a person's heart rate, for example, these devices can [5]_____ a person's health. This information can help the [6]_____, nurse, or doctor take care of patients better.

B Complete the sentences. Circle the correct words.

1 The (**treatment** / **healthcare**) for a bad back involves lots of rest.
2 There is still no (**cure** / **caregiver**) for many types of cancer.
3 People who are overweight and don't exercise are likely to (**suffer from** / **cure**) health issues.
4 Many fitness (**treatments** / **wearables**) monitor things such as the number of steps people take.
5 Devices that track exercise can help (**monitor** / **motivate**) people to be more active.

C Work with a partner. Discuss these questions.

1 Does your country have a high percentage of elderly people?
2 Are there any special healthcare services for them?

LISTENING My health routine

> **Talking about the benefits of something**
> We can use expressions like the ones below to describe the benefits of something.
> *It's great for …*   *It works well for people who …*   *I find … most useful.*

A ▶ **3.3** Watch Kate Chong talk about her health routine. Check (✓) the ways she stays healthy.

- ☐ by getting enough rest
- ☐ by having a balanced diet
- ☐ by cycling to work every day
- ☐ by exercising every weekend

B ▶ **3.3** Watch again. Complete the sentences. Circle the correct words.

1 Chong uses a running app on her phone to keep track of
 (**the weather conditions on each run** / **how far she's run**).

2 She likes the app because it
 (**is easy to use** / **helps her stay disciplined**).

3 Chong's cycling app allows her to
 (**compare cycling data with friends** / **train with a virtual cycling partner**).

Kate Chong leads an active lifestyle.

C **CRITICAL THINKING**

Reflecting Work with a partner. What other ways do you think technology can help improve people's health?

SPEAKING Talking about staying healthy

A ▶ **3.4** Is Speaker A motivated to keep fit?

A: You seem pretty fit. Do you do any regular exercise?

B: Yeah. I go to the gym a few times a week.

A: What do you do there?

B: I do some stretching and then usually run for half an hour or so.

A: Don't you get bored? How do you motivate yourself?

B: Well, I often go with a friend. Also, I recently bought a wearable. It helps me learn more about my lifestyle habits, and motivates me to do more. How about you? Do you do much exercise?

A: Not very often. I'm usually too tired after work. Maybe I should sign up for a class at the gym. I think that will make me more motivated!

B Practice the conversation with a partner.

C Work with a partner. Talk about what you do to keep fit, how you motivate yourself, and if you use any technology to keep track of your health. Use the expressions in blue above to help you.

> Do you do any regular exercise?

> I try to go swimming every week.

3B Tech in healthcare

LANGUAGE FOCUS Discussing mobile healthcare

A ▶ 3.5 Read the information. Do you look up health-related information online? What do you look for?

HEALTHCARE IS GOING MOBILE
Technology is changing the way we monitor and manage our health.

52% of smartphone users now gather health-related information on their phones.

More than **25%** of doctors are using mobile technology to provide patient care.

As a result of cheaper and more accurate sensors, the smart wearable healthcare market will be worth more than $40 billion dollars by 2020.

2014 **$2 billion**

2020 **$41 billion**

Almost **50%** of people aged 25–44 will be using wearable devices by 2018.

Over **75 million** wearable devices will be sold between 2014 and 2020.

B ▶ 3.6 Listen to the conversation. What does the woman recommend her friend to do? Discuss with a partner.

C ▶ 3.7 Watch and study the language in the chart.

> **Talking about cause and effect**
>
> Obesity can lead to other health problems, so it's important to have a healthy diet.
>
> Health apps are becoming popular nowadays because people are more concerned about their health.
>
> Elderly people usually require more medical care due to age-related illnesses.
>
> You should eat less red meat, as too much of it can lead to heart disease.
>
> As a result of improvements in medical technology, we are able to treat more illnesses.
>
> Gathering personal health information has become easier because of the Internet.

For more information on **cause and effect**, see Grammar Summary 3 on page 184.

D ▶ **3.6** Listen to the conversation in **B** again. Complete the sentences from the conversation.

1 "I had a terrible night's sleep _____ I kept waking up."

2 "I can't really focus in class sometimes _____ I'm so tired."

3 "You'll get to know your sleep habits, _____ you can see what helps you sleep."

E Match the two parts of the sentences.

1 A lot of people are buying wearables   ○   ○ so they're easy to carry around.

2 Many lives are saved each year   ○   ○ people can find out a lot more about their health.

3 Fitness devices are usually small and light,   ○   ○ because of improvements in medical technology.

4 As a result of improvements in mobile healthcare,   ○   ○ because they are interested in monitoring their health.

F ▶ **3.8** Complete the information. Circle the correct words. Then listen and check your answers.

Michael Lwin is a Burmese-American who moved back to Myanmar in 2012. When Lwin met his cousin Yar Zar Minn Htoo in Myanmar, he found out that his cousin had gotten hepatitis B—a serious disease—¹(**so** / **because**) a rural doctor had used dirty needles and infected Yar Zar Minn Htoo with the virus.

Lwin and Yar Zar Minn Htoo wanted to improve people's access to healthcare in their country, ²(**so** / **as**) in 2012, they worked together to start Koe Koe Tech. They created Kyan Mar Yae—the country's first general health app—which sends personalized messages to users' phones. ³(**As** / **Because of**) more than 90 percent of the population in Myanmar use smartphones, this is an effective way to provide more people with access to healthcare information and advice. According to Lwin, this app will also benefit the women and children of Myanmar, ⁴(**due to** / **as**) 70 percent of births take place outside a hospital.

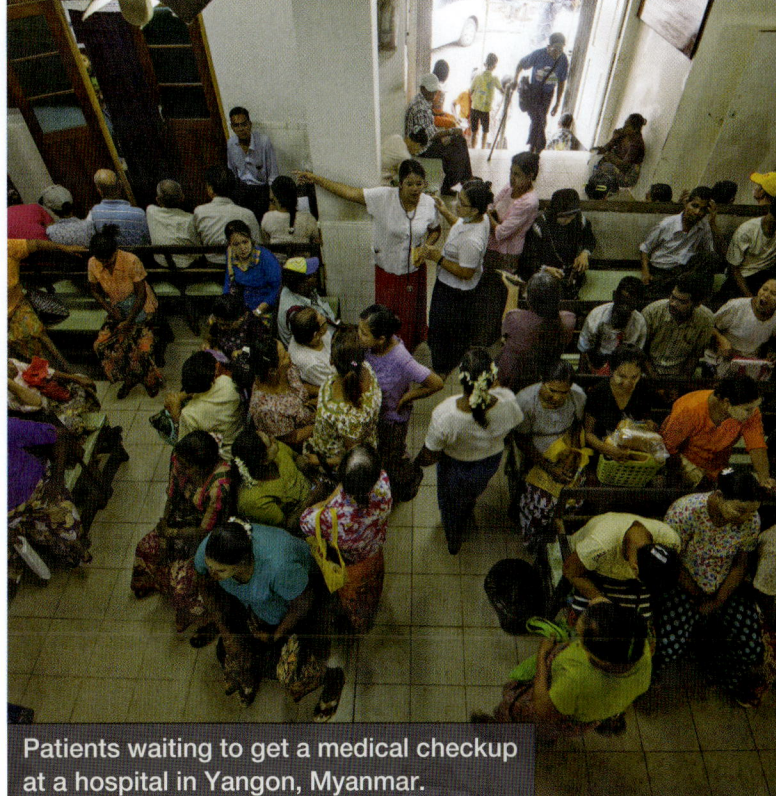

Patients waiting to get a medical checkup at a hospital in Yangon, Myanmar.

SPEAKING Talking about healthcare tech

Work with a partner. You are going to read about a type of healthcare technology that could be used in the future. **Student A:** Turn to page 165. **Student B:** Turn to page 166. Describe the technology you have read about to your partner, and explain the effects it could have on people in the future.

3C The challenge of Alzheimer's

PRE-READING Predicting

Skim the first paragraph. What kinds of challenges do you think there are in countries where people live longer?

▶ 3.9

1   For the first time in history, there are more people above the age of 65 than children below the age of five. As populations grow older, aging societies will begin to face major challenges—such as the provision of healthcare.

    Elderly people have a higher chance of suffering from illnesses such as diabetes, cancer, and heart disease. Providing proper healthcare facilities and treatment is expensive, and the rising cost of healthcare puts a lot of **pressure** on the working population. In Europe, for example, there are currently four working people supporting one elderly person. By 2050, this number will fall to two workers per elderly person.

    One common health problem that affects elderly people is Alzheimer's disease. Alzheimer's—the most common type of dementia—affects a person's memory, **behavior**, and thinking. Because of memory loss and behavioral changes, people with Alzheimer's may slowly become unable to take care of themselves, eventually requiring **constant** care from family members or caregivers.

    There is no cure for Alzheimer's at the moment—drugs can only treat its symptoms.

Many developed countries are experiencing aging populations. One of the most notable examples is Japan. Japan's population is rapidly aging as a result of fewer babies being born and people living longer. By 2060, four in ten people will be over the age of 65.

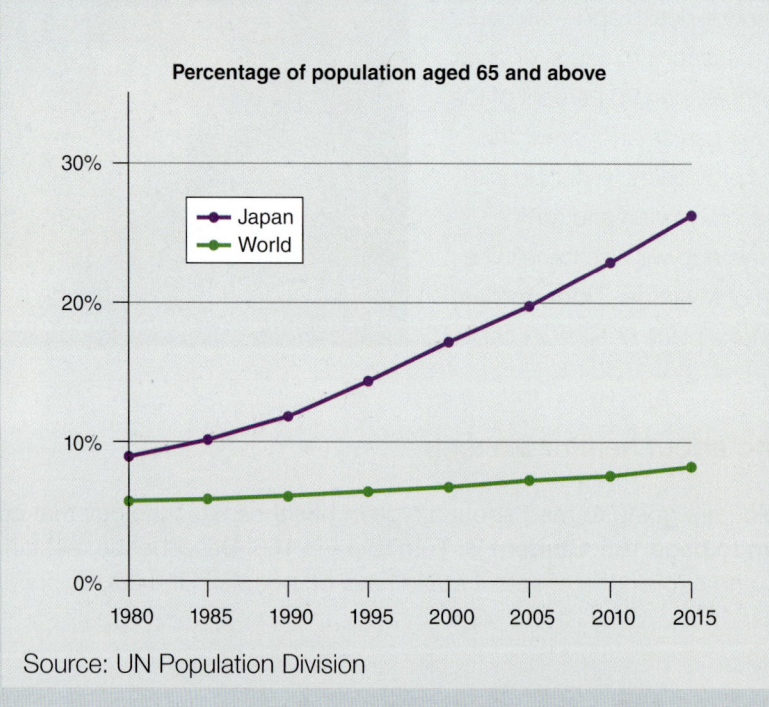

Percentage of population aged 65 and above

Source: UN Population Division

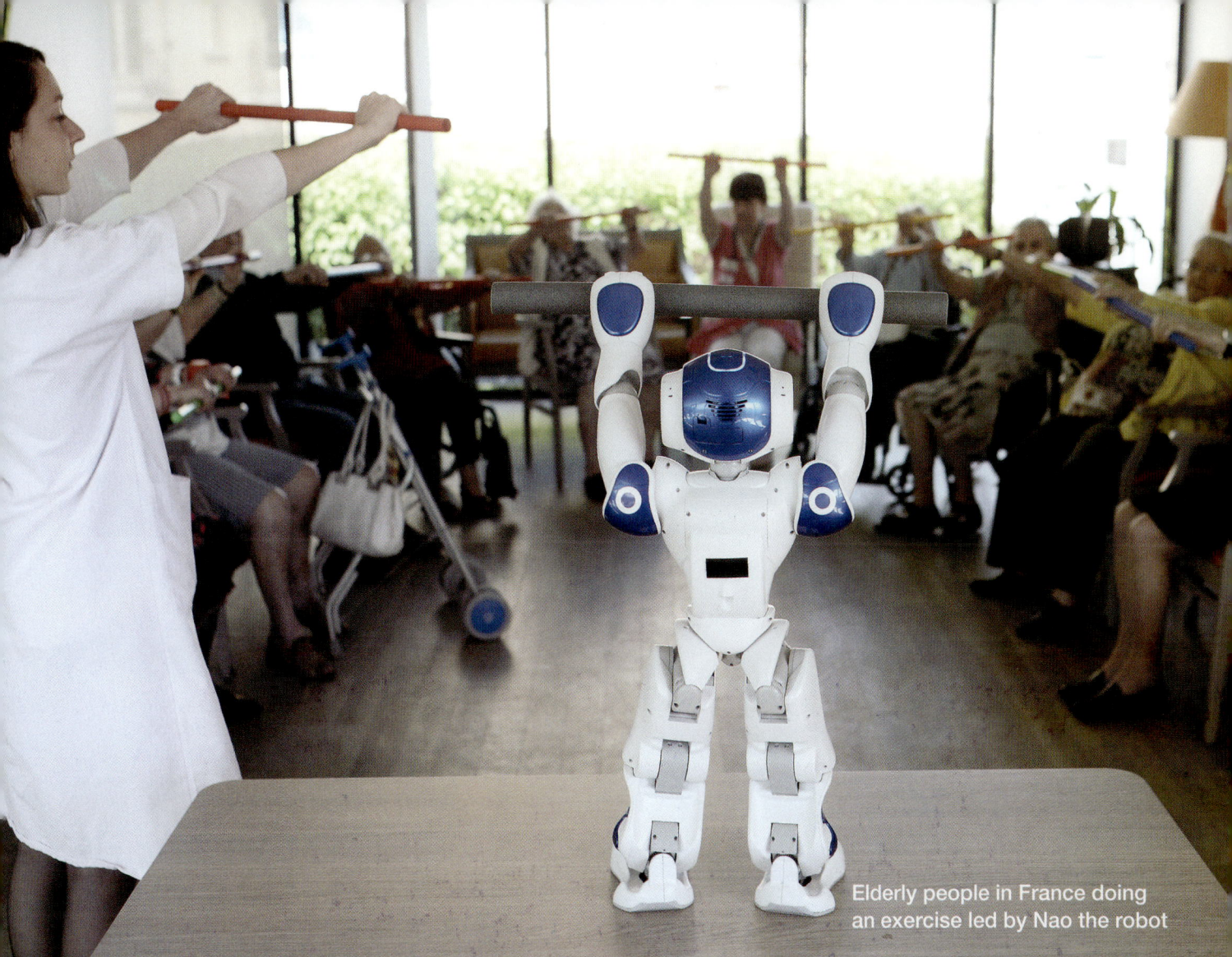

Elderly people in France doing an exercise led by Nao the robot

25 But technology can improve the lives of those living with the condition by making it easier for them to go about their daily activities. For example, tracking devices placed in watches or jewelry can monitor where a person is. Automated[1] reminders can also 30 be stored in motion sensors and placed around the house. When a sensor detects movement, it can play a recorded voice message to remind the person to lock the door or turn off the stove.

Alzheimer's disease is a huge challenge, but 35 we may be getting close to finding a solution. In the future, it might be possible to treat Alzheimer's without using drugs. A team of researchers in Australia has created a form of technology that can send sound waves into the brain. These 40 sound waves help to clear waste in the brain that contributes to Alzheimer's. The team has tested their technology and found that it helped to restore[2] memory in 75 percent of mice. Work on the technology isn't complete, but, if successful, 45 it could **prevent** memory loss in people with Alzheimer's. "I think this really does fundamentally change our understanding of how to treat this disease," says Professor Jürgen Götz, a co-author of the study, "and I foresee a great future for this 50 **approach**."

[1] **automated:** *adj.* run by a machine or computer
[2] **restore:** *v.* to return something to its original state

UNDERSTANDING MAIN IDEAS

What is the main idea of the passage?

    a There is a need to better understand the cause of Alzheimer's disease.

    b Technology may be able to help tackle some of the problems of people with Alzheimer's.

    c Many elderly people are unable to afford the cost of treating Alzheimer's.

UNDERSTANDING CAUSE AND EFFECT

Complete the diagram showing causes and effects.

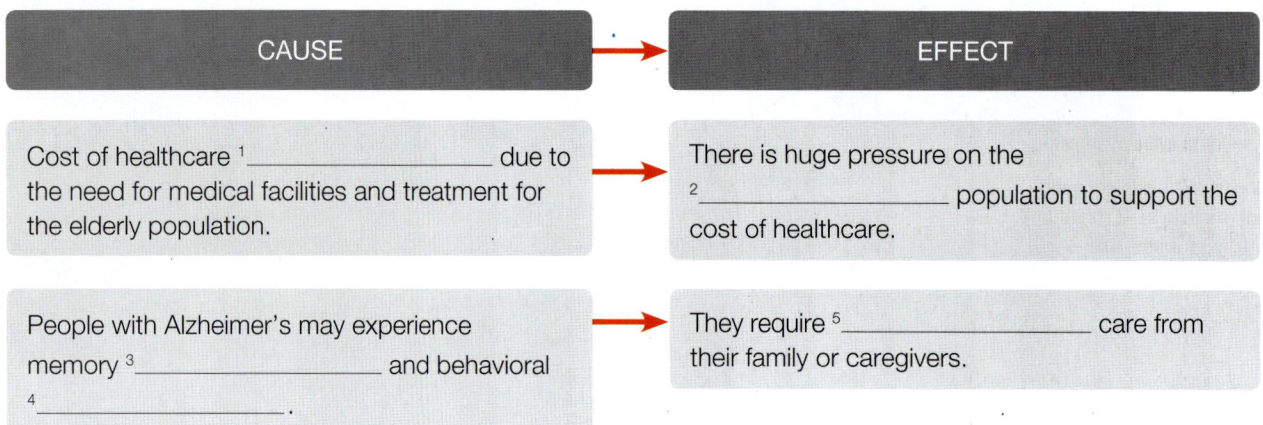

CAUSE	EFFECT
Cost of healthcare 1_____ due to the need for medical facilities and treatment for the elderly population.	There is huge pressure on the 2_____ population to support the cost of healthcare.
People with Alzheimer's may experience memory 3_____ and behavioral 4_____.	They require 5_____ care from their family or caregivers.

UNDERSTANDING DETAILS

Choose the correct option to complete each sentence.

    1 Alzheimer's is a disease that mainly affects the _____.

        a muscles   **b** blood   **c** brain

    2 Australian researchers have shown that it may be possible to _____ people with Alzheimer's.

        a prevent memory loss in   **b** increase the sleep quality of   **c** improve the communication ability of

BUILDING VOCABULARY

A Complete the sentences using the words in blue from the passage.

    1 Researchers are still finding ways to _____ people from getting cancer.

    2 Family members are often under a lot of _____ caring for people with Alzheimer's.

    3 A _____ decrease in the birth rate can cause populations to shrink.

    4 When an idea doesn't work well, you should try a different _____.

    5 Scientists sometimes study the _____ of animals to find out what we can learn from them.

B CRITICAL THINKING

    Inferring What is the author's attitude toward finding solutions to the challenges of Alzheimer's? What evidence is there from the article?

3D My simple invention, designed to keep my grandfather safe

TEDTALKS

KENNETH SHINOZUKA has been designing smart products since he was six years old. Ever since his grandfather was **diagnosed** with Alzheimer's disease, Kenneth's family has **struggled** to care for him. **Concerned** by this, Kenneth designed a smart device. The **sensor** in the device **detects** pressure when someone steps on it.

Kenneth Shinozuka's idea worth spreading is that smart uses of sensory technology can improve our lives as we age—particularly for Alzheimer's patients and those who care for them.

PREVIEWING

Read the paragraphs above. Match each **bold** word to its meaning. You will hear these words in the TED Talk.

1 worried _____
2 notices something _____
3 had difficulty _____
4 identified a medical condition _____
5 a device that responds to things like light or sound _____

VIEWING

A ▶ **3.10** Watch Part 1 of the TED Talk. Choose the correct options.

1 Kenneth's grandfather's condition brought a lot of stress to his family because he often _____.
   a couldn't go to sleep
   b wandered off by himself
   c couldn't express his thoughts

2 Kenneth was worried about his aunt's well-being because she was _____.
   a not eating healthy meals
   b often getting sick
   c not getting enough rest at night

B ▶ **3.11** Watch Part 2 of the TED Talk. Complete the labels describing how Kenneth Shinozuka's invention works. Then number the steps from 1–4.

1 Patient puts sock on.

2 When the patient _____ on the floor, the pressure sensor detects a(n) _____ in pressure.

3 Sensor sends a wireless alert to the caregiver's _____.

4 Smartphone makes a(n) _____.

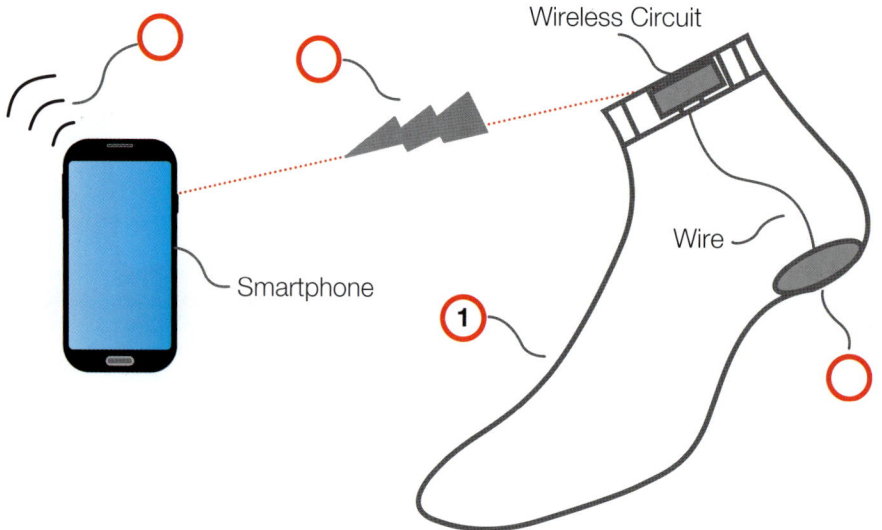

C ▶ **3.12** Watch Part 3 of the TED Talk. Complete the diagram showing Kenneth Shinozuka's invention and research process.

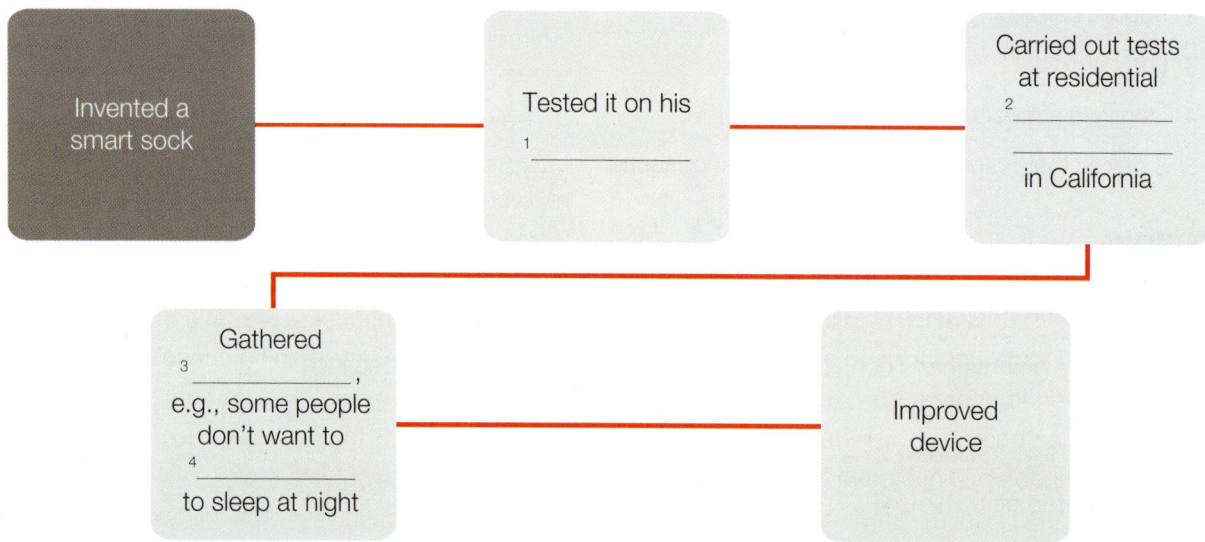

D CRITICAL THINKING

Inferring Work with a partner. Look at the quote below. What other correlations would you look for?

"I'm currently examining correlations between the frequency of a patient's nightly wandering and his or her daily activities and diet."

VOCABULARY IN CONTEXT

A ▶ **3.13** Watch the excerpts from the TED Talk. Choose the correct meaning of the words.

B Complete the sentences with the words from the box.

| firsthand | stem from | incorporate | keep an eye on | overwhelming |

1 Caregivers or family members need to _____ people with Alzheimer's.
2 Some medical conditions such as obesity may _____ bad lifestyle choices.
3 There is _____ evidence that smoking causes lung cancer.
4 Inventors have to _____ feedback from users to improve their creations.
5 Many caregivers experience _____ how hard it is for people with Alzheimer's to get on with daily life.

PRESENTATION SKILLS Opening with interesting facts

> Start your presentation with interesting facts to get your audience's attention.
> *Did you know that …?*   *You may not know that …*
> *Here is a fact you may not know …*   *What do you think …?*

▶ **3.14** Watch part of Kenneth Shinozuka's TED Talk. Complete the facts he gives.

1 "What's the _____ threat to Americans' health? Cancer? Heart attacks? Diabetes? The answer is actually none of these; it's Alzheimer's disease."

2 "Every _____, someone in the United States is diagnosed with Alzheimer's."

3 "As the number of Alzheimer's patients _____ by the year 2050, caring for them, as well as the rest of the aging population, will become an overwhelming societal challenge."

Kenneth Shinozuka hopes to turn his invention into a product that can help people with Alzheimer's.

3E Healthcare solutions

COMMUNICATE Innovative healthcare solutions

A Work in small groups. Choose one of the scenarios below.

> **Scenario A**
> Person A is 70 years old. He is no longer able to walk more than a few meters on his own. He lives alone and is finding basic chores like cleaning and shopping very difficult.
>
> **Scenario B**
> Person B is 65 years old. She needs to take medicine regularly as she suffers from several medical conditions. However, she often forgets to take the medicine. Sometimes she even takes the wrong medicine or the wrong amount.
>
> **Scenario C**
> Person C is a 24-year-old athlete. He is training for a competition next month. He has to keep to a strict, healthy diet in order to be at his best during the competition. However, his training schedules are very busy and he doesn't have enough time to plan his meals properly.

B In your group, brainstorm possible tech solutions that could help make life easier for the person. Think about the problem the person faces, how it affects his or her daily life, and how technology can help.

C Take turns explaining your group's scenario and presenting your tech solution to the class. Then vote for the most innovative idea.

> **Talking about problems and solutions**
> He finds it difficult to …   This … can aid the person in …
> He struggles with …   One way to improve the situation is …

> The person in our scenario faces the problem of …

> He can use this tech product to help with …

WRITING Expressing an opinion

Write a short letter to a company that develops tech products for healthcare purposes. Explain the healthcare issue you discussed above, giving your opinion on the best actions to help with similar cases.

> Elderly people who live alone may need some help in their daily lives. A possible way to help them is …

Tech products such as this software for medical students can help improve the quality of healthcare.

Presentation 1

MODEL PRESENTATION

A Complete the transcript of the presentation using the words in the box.

| finished | because | going to tell | will make |
| did you know | so | spent | ends up |

Hi. I'm Lori. It's nice to be here today. ¹_____ that in the Pacific Ocean, there's a huge body of plastic trash floating around that's twice the size of Texas? We have a really big problem with trash in the world. Today, I'm ²_____ you about what I do to help and how you can get involved, too.

A lot of trash ³_____ on the beach, in rivers, or in the sea. All this trash harms humans and wildlife ⁴_____ it pollutes our environment and poisons our food sources. I live near the sea, ⁵_____ I decided to volunteer for a beach clean-up a few Sundays ago. There were about 20 of us. We had our own buckets and gloves, and ⁶_____ a couple of hours picking up all the trash. Here's a picture of the trash we collected. And this picture shows how the beach looked when we ⁷_____. Seeing the clean beach at the end was really satisfying. It was fun, too, and I made some new friends.

So, that's how I help. I can only play a small role, of course, but when lots of people join in, it makes a big difference. I encourage you to try a clean-up. It's fun, easy to do, and worthwhile. And you ⁸_____ new friends, too. Thanks for listening.

B ▶ P.1 Watch the presentation and check your answers.

C ▶ P.1 Review the list of presentation skills from Units 1–3 below. Which does the speaker use? Check (✓) them as you watch again. Then compare with a partner.

The speaker …
- helps the audience visualize by
  - doing a demonstration ☐
  - giving interesting facts ☐
  - telling a story ☐
- using visuals ☐
- comments on visuals ☐
- opens with an interesting fact ☐

D ▶ P.1 Do you remember the way Lori draws attention to the visuals? Complete the sentences below. Then watch and check. Notice her gestures.

"_____ of the trash we collected. And _____ how the beach looked when we finished."

YOUR TURN

A You are going to plan and give a short presentation about how you can make a difference. Think about what you want to do, and make notes in the box below.

> How I can make a difference
>
> Why I think it can help

B Look at the useful phrases in the box below. Think about which ones you will need in your presentation.

> **Useful phrases**
>
> Beginning: It's great to be here today.
> Did you know that …?
> I'm going to … / I'd like to …
>
> Commenting on visuals: This picture shows …
> Here's a picture of …
>
> Concluding: So, in conclusion, …
> I encourage you to …
> Thanks for listening.

C Work with a partner. Take turns giving your presentation using your notes. Use some of the presentation skills from Units 1–3. As you listen, check (✓) each skill your partner uses.

> The speaker …
> - helps the audience visualize by
>   - doing a demonstration ☐
>   - giving interesting facts ☐
>   - telling a story ☐
>   - using visuals ☐
> - comments on visuals ☐
> - opens with an interesting fact ☐

D Give your partner some feedback on their talk. Include at least two things you liked and one thing that could be improved.

> That was a great presentation. You gave interesting facts and included beautiful pictures. Maybe you could talk a bit more about the pictures.

4 Designing the Web

“ Consider the fact that Google processes over one billion search queries every day, that every minute, over 100 hours of footage are uploaded to YouTube. ”

Margaret Gould Stewart
User experience designer, TED speaker

UNIT GOALS

In this unit, you will …
- talk about digital products and how they are designed.
- read about designing websites for millions of people.
- watch a TED Talk about designing for all kinds of users.

WARM UP

▶ **4.1** Watch part of Margaret Gould Stewart's TED Talk. Answer the questions with a partner.

1 What examples of classic design can you think of?
2 What do you think Stewart means by designs that "live inside your pocket"?

4A Technology and design

VOCABULARY Describing website features

A ▶ 4.2 Complete the labels using the words in the box. Then listen and check your answers.

| search | browse | review | download |
| rate | button | log in | logo |

This is the website's
1 _____ .

Use the 2 _____
box to look for posts you're interested in.

Enter your user name
and password to
3 _____ .

You can
4 _____
the sidebar for
the latest posts.

Click on the "share"
5 _____
to send the link to
someone else.

You can 6 _____
the recipe by clicking on this icon.

Click on one of these icons to
7 _____ the post.

Click to read the
8 _____
of a café.

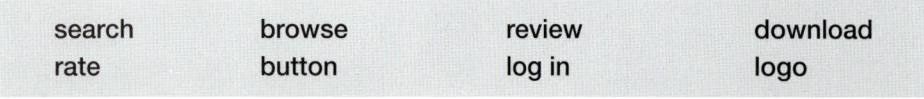

B Complete the sentences. Circle the correct words.

1 McDonald's golden arches and Starbucks's mermaid are examples of famous (**logos** / **buttons**).

2 A lot of people go online to write (**downloads** / **reviews**) of the products they buy.

3 Customers usually (**rate** / **log in**) a product based on price and how user-friendly it is.

4 It's easy to look for information by (**downloading** / **browsing**) the Web.

C Work with a partner. What kinds of apps do you usually download? Have you ever written an online review?

> I usually download news apps. I like to keep up with current events.

> I prefer downloading gaming apps. My favorite is …

LISTENING Designing websites

> **Stating your points**
> Here are some commonly used phrases for listing points.
> First/Second, ...   Also, ...   One other thing is ...

A ▶ **4.3** Watch web designer Carrie Cousins talk about the work she does. How does she define "user experience"? Discuss with a partner.

B ▶ **4.4** Watch Cousins talk about the things she focuses on when designing a website. Match them to their explanations.

1 functionality ○   ○ The content is nice to look at.
2 readability   ○   ○ The website solves a user problem.
3 usability   ○   ○ The website is easy to navigate.

C CRITICAL THINKING

Evaluating Work with a partner. What other things do you think are important to consider when designing a website? Why?

Carrie Cousins has more than 15 years of experience in the media industry.

SPEAKING Talking about making decisions

A ▶ **4.5** How did Speaker B decide what product to buy?

A: Hey, is that a new tablet? I didn't know you had one.
B: Yeah, I looked around and finally decided on this one.
A: It looks great. How did you decide which one to get?
B: Well, I checked out the company's website and watched their promotional videos. I also read a lot of reviews online.
A: Did you compare prices?
B: Yeah, this model is the best, I think. It's not the most expensive, and it has pretty good features for the price.
A: What do you like most about it?
B: The size. It's smaller than standard tablets, so I can easily carry it around.

B Practice the conversation with a partner.

C Work with a partner. Think of something you bought recently and describe your experience. Use the expressions in blue above to help you.

> I bought a new pair of earphones over the weekend.
> How did you decide which ones to get?
> I looked around online and then ...

4B User experience

LANGUAGE FOCUS Discussing the influence of user reviews

A ▶ **4.6** Read the information. How often do you buy something online? How important are user reviews to you?

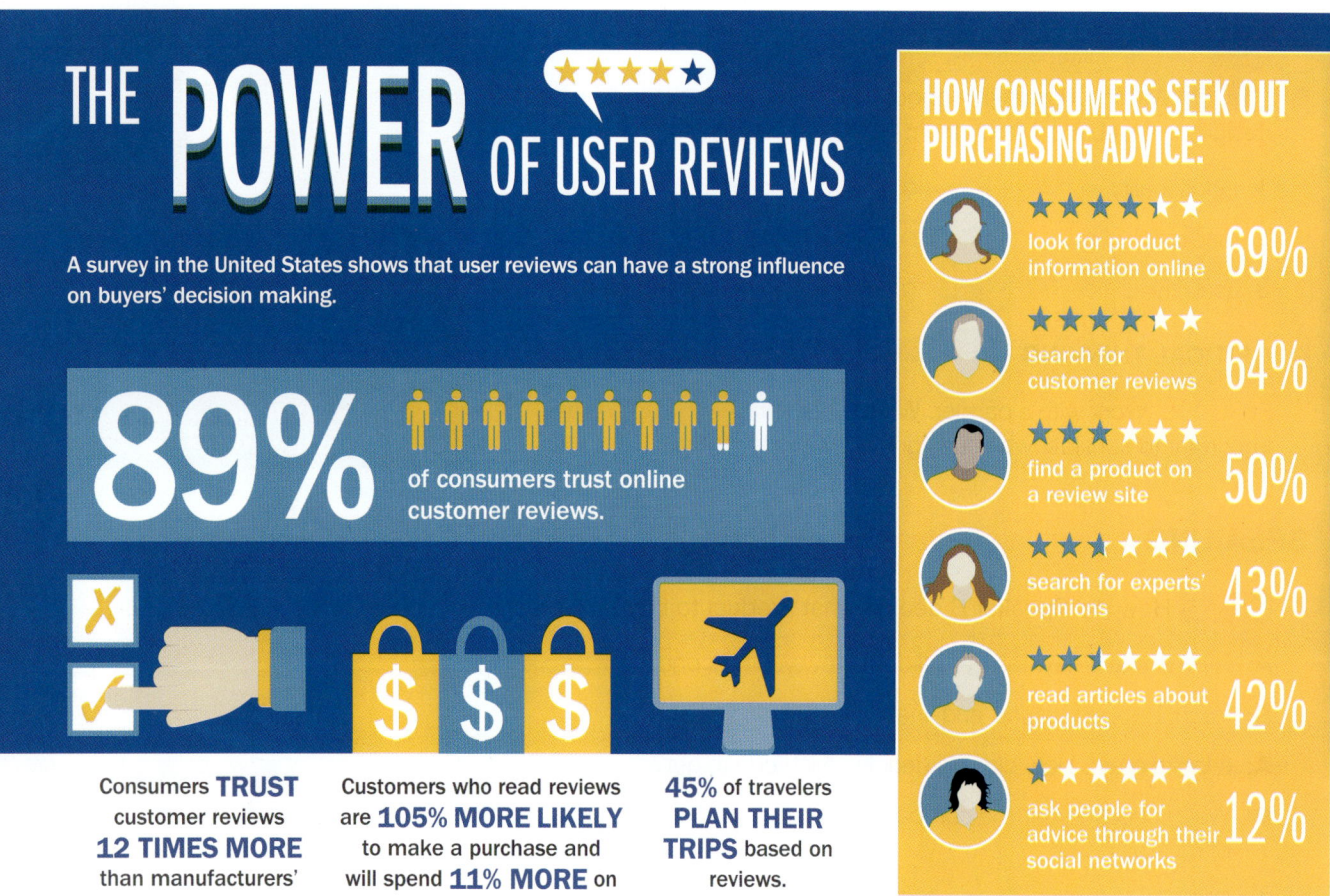

THE POWER OF USER REVIEWS

A survey in the United States shows that user reviews can have a strong influence on buyers' decision making.

89% of consumers trust online customer reviews.

Consumers **TRUST** customer reviews **12 TIMES MORE** than manufacturers' descriptions.

Customers who read reviews are **105% MORE LIKELY** to make a purchase and will spend **11% MORE** on that product.

45% of travelers **PLAN THEIR TRIPS** based on reviews.

HOW CONSUMERS SEEK OUT PURCHASING ADVICE:

- look for product information online — 69%
- search for customer reviews — 64%
- find a product on a review site — 50%
- search for experts' opinions — 43%
- read articles about products — 42%
- ask people for advice through their social networks — 12%

B ▶ **4.7** Listen to the conversation. What do the speakers decide to do? Discuss with a partner.

C ▶ **4.8** Watch and study the language in the chart.

Comparing products and services

I think using a navigation app is *easier than* looking at a printed map.

I think it's *much more efficient* to work on a desktop *than* on a tablet computer.

Many consumers search online for *the best* product available before buying.

Some smartphones are *just as expensive as* laptops these days.

These days, people use their phones in *very different* ways *from* just ten years ago.

Smartphones today have pretty much *the same* functions *as* computers.

For more information on **making comparisons**, see Grammar Summary 4 on pages 184–185.

D ▶ **4.7** Listen to the conversation in **B** again. Circle the correct words.

1 The woman is (**as confident as** / **more confident than**) the man about the reliability of online reviews.

2 The man thinks that checking out the restaurant in person is (**better than** / **not as good as**) reading online reviews.

E Complete the sentences to make comparisons. Add suitable comparison words as necessary.

1 Sometimes, cheaper products may be just _____ (reliable) more expensive products—the price may not mean a difference in quality.

2 One of the _____ (important) things in website design is making it easy for users to find information.

3 Online prices are usually _____ (not, expensive) store prices.

4 I bought a shirt online, but when it arrived, it was _____ (different) how it looked in the pictures.

5 Some people think shopping at an actual store is _____ (good) buying things online because they can touch and try out the products.

F ▶ **4.9** Complete the information. Circle the correct words. Then listen and check your answers.

It has become a lot ¹(**more** / **better**) common for consumers to look for reviews online when making decisions on what to buy. It helps them find out what other people think of a restaurant or an item they have bought. According to a survey, consumers think that customer reviews are 12 times ²(**more trustworthy than** / **most trustworthy**) the manufacturer's product description. The growing influence of online reviews means that businesses have to work hard to provide the ³(**better** / **best**) products to stay competitive. Online comparison sites also make it ⁴(**as easy as** / **easier than**) before for consumers to compare prices. They can quickly find out if a business is charging them ⁵(**as different as** / **the same as**) others for a product or service.

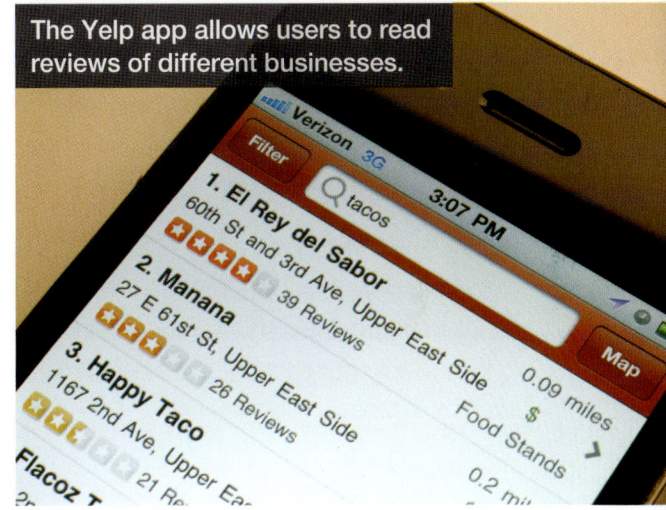

The Yelp app allows users to read reviews of different businesses.

SPEAKING Making decisions based on user reviews

A Work with a partner. You are planning to buy a virtual reality headset. Turn to page 168 and read the reviews of two products. Discuss the following questions.

1 What features do you think are most important?

2 How do the products compare in terms of the features you're looking for?

B Decide which product you would buy. Describe the product you chose and give reasons for your choice.

> I chose number 1. It's lighter and cheaper, so …

> Having a lot of features is good, but the price …

4C Website design on a giant scale

PRE-READING Skimming

Skim the article. The purpose of the article is to _____.

a explain how difficult it is to design huge websites
b discuss some lessons in huge website design
c explore the common challenges of digital design

1 Margaret Gould Stewart has designed for some of the giants of the Internet, including Google, YouTube, and Facebook. Here are two lessons she has learned 5 from her experience designing for Internet users.

LOOK BEYOND DATA

For a long time, Facebook had a tool that allowed people to report photos as **spam** or abuse.[1] But of the cases reported, only a small percentage of 10 the photos were actually offensive.[2] One of the designers on the team felt there probably was a reason for this, so he studied the cases carefully. He found that in most cases users just didn't like the photos of themselves their friends had posted, 15 and wanted them taken down. To enable people to report cases like these, the Facebook team added a new feature. This feature allowed people to message their friends to ask them to take the photo down. But only 20 percent of people used 20 the function.

The team worked on the case further—it spoke to communications experts and studied rules of polite language. It discovered that users didn't just want to tell their friends to take the 25 photo down—they wanted to tell their friends how the photo made them feel. So the team made a small change. People could select a message to explain why they didn't like it, such as, "It's embarrassing." This small change had a huge 30 **impact**—60 percent of people who reported photos used the function. Surveys showed that people on both sides of the conversation felt better as a result.

While data about how people are using a 35 product can help designers make decisions, it isn't always as simple as following the numbers. Other factors such as intuition,[3] research, and testing of design are equally important. As Stewart points out, "Data can help you make a 40 good design great, but it will never make a bad design good."

Mark Zuckerberg, CEO of Facebook, introducing the new features of its messaging app

INTRODUCE CHANGE CAREFULLY

At one time, YouTube was looking for ways to **encourage** more people to rate videos. When
[45] Stewart and her team looked into the data, they found that most people were only using either the highest rating (five stars) or the lowest rating (one star). Almost no one was using two, three, or four stars. So the team decided to simplify the rating—it
[50] gave users a choice between good or bad: thumbs up or thumbs down.

YouTube tried to prepare people for this change by sharing data about how the five-star rating system wasn't being used as intended. It
[55] announced that it was going to change the system to match user behavior. When the change was made, it was still **frustrating** for some users as they had become **attached** to the old design. However, because of the preparatory steps taken earlier, it
[60] was easier for YouTube to get users to accept the change.

This experience shows that even when huge websites try to manage change carefully, it's impossible to completely avoid negative responses.
[65] Any changes—even small improvements—need to be introduced carefully.

---

[1] **abuse:** *n.* improper use of something
[2] **offensive:** *adj.* making someone feel hurt or uncomfortable
[3] **intuition:** *n.* a natural feeling about something

SUMMARIZING KEY POINTS

Complete the diagram summarizing Margaret Gould Stewart's experiences.

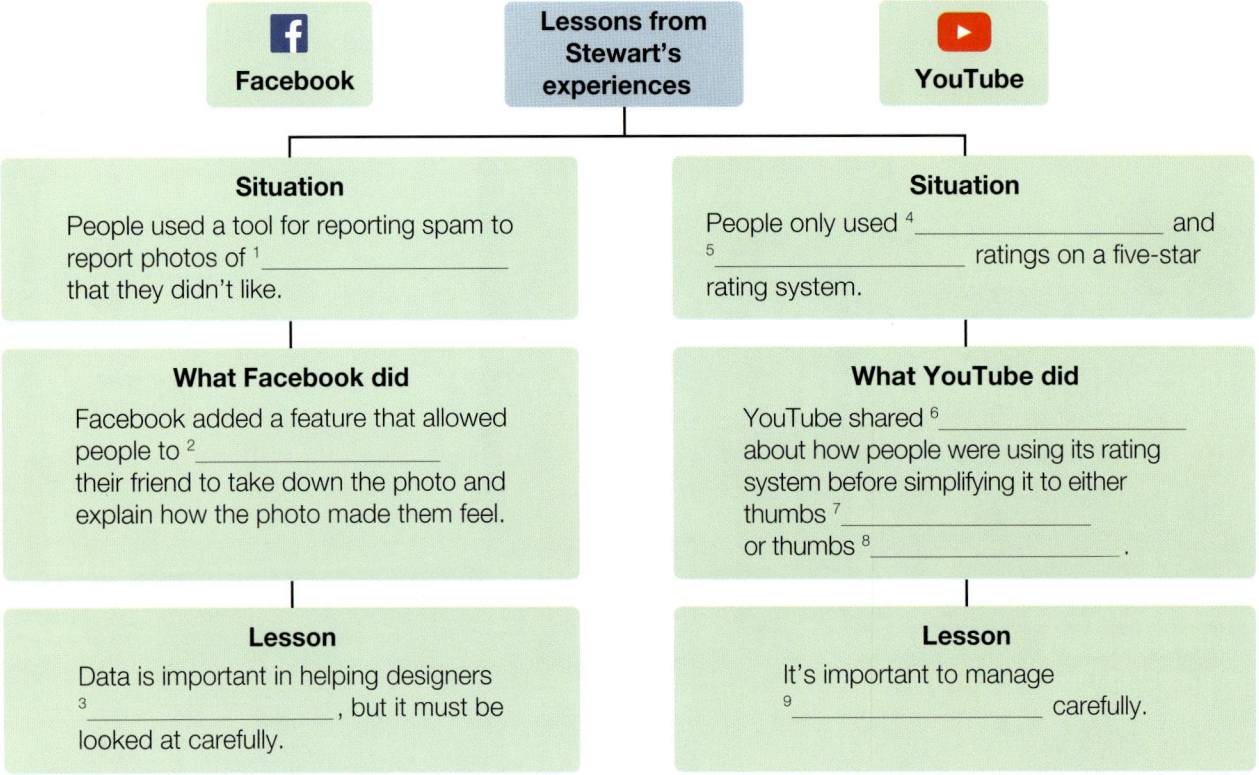

BUILDING VOCABULARY

A Match the words in blue from the passage to their definitions.

1. spam — an effect
2. impact — having a strong liking for something
3. encourage — unwanted emails
4. frustrating — annoying, irritating
5. attached — to make someone more likely to do something

B Complete the sentences using the words in A.

1. I get more _____ than regular emails.
2. YouTube made its rating system simpler to _____ more people to rate videos.
3. Creative innovations can have a big _____ on how people interact with one another.
4. Some people may find learning how to use a new cell phone a(n) _____ experience.
5. Many people become emotionally _____ to their smartphones.

C CRITICAL THINKING

Inferring Why do you think more people sent a message to their friend after Facebook allowed them to explain how the photo made them feel? Discuss with a partner.

4D How giant websites design for you (and a billion others, too)

TEDTALKS

MARGARET GOULD STEWART has spent her career asking the question, "How do we design user experiences that change the world?" She has managed user experiences for some of the most visited websites in the world, including YouTube and Facebook. The wide reach of these websites means that Stewart has had to deal with **unprecedented** challenges and **constraints**.

Margaret Gould Stewart's idea worth spreading is that designing at a global **scale** requires both the **audacity** to believe your product is needed by the whole world, and the **humility** to understand that your audience is far more important than you as a designer.

PREVIEWING

Read the paragraphs above. Match each **bold** word to its meaning. You will hear these words in the TED Talk.

1. the quality of not being proud _____
2. confidence or courage to take risks _____
3. the size or level of something _____
4. things that limit what you can do _____
5. not done before or hasn't happened in the past _____

VIEWING

A ▶ **4.11** Watch Part 1 of the TED Talk. Check (✓) the sentences about design challenges that Margaret Gould Stewart mentions.

☐ Designers need to believe that their products are something the world wants.

☐ Users differ greatly in the kinds of things they want.

☐ Designers must understand that their work may have an important impact on people's lives.

☐ There are no fixed ways of doing things or guaranteed success when designing at scale.

B ▶ **4.12** Watch Part 2 of the TED Talk. Which of the following describes the lesson learned from designing the Facebook "Like" button?

   a When you are designing on a huge scale, every detail—no matter how small it seems—is important.

   b It's necessary to spend a lot of time and effort redesigning elements many times in order to make sure that the overall design fits the brand image.

   c The smallest design details are the most important when designing on a huge scale, and you need to get the best designers to work on them.

C ▶ **4.13** Watch Part 3 of the TED Talk. Check (✓) the information Margaret Gould Stewart is likely to agree with.

People who design at scale _____.

☐ need to design for low-end cell phones

☐ should try using their products in different languages

☐ need to try out their products on both old and new phones

☐ should find ways to cut costs

D CRITICAL THINKING

Inferring Margaret Gould Stewart describes her work as something that isn't always glamorous. What does this say about the work she does?

“ If you want to design for the whole world, you have to design for where people are, and not where you are. ”

VOCABULARY IN CONTEXT

A ▶ **4.14** Watch the excerpts from the TED Talk. Choose the correct meaning of the words.

B Complete the sentences. Circle the correct words.

1 Designers can (**get their heads around** / **keep in touch with**) clients via email or social media.

2 Great designs are (**timeless** / **out of sync**)—they last forever.

3 Designers for huge websites should always (**keep in mind** / **get their heads around**) that change needs to be managed carefully.

4 It can be difficult to (**get your head around** / **keep in mind**) complicated computer terms unless they're explained simply.

5 I haven't done any design work in a while. I think I'm (**out of sync** / **keeping in touch**) with the latest trends in design.

PRESENTATION SKILLS Asking the audience questions

> Ask your audience questions to keep them engaged and to encourage them to think about the topic. Questions sometimes begin with *So* or *Now*.

A ▶ **4.15** Watch part of Margaret Gould Stewart's TED Talk. Complete the questions she uses in her talk.

1 "What do you think of when _____?"

2 "Now, why would we spend so much time on _____?"

3 "So how do we keep this _____?"

4 "So what does it mean to _____?"

B Work with a partner. Take turns explaining the steps for doing something. Practice using questions in your explanation.

> Do you often receive spam? Here's how you can prevent …

4E Making suggestions

COMMUNICATE Improving user experiences

A Work in groups. Think of a website you've used that could be better designed. Brainstorm ways to improve the design to create a better user experience. Consider the following questions.

What's good about the website? _____
_____

What doesn't work so well? Why? _____
_____

How can it be redesigned to make it better for people to use? _____
_____

B Describe the website your group chose to the class and suggest ways it can be improved.

> **Describing user experience**
> *The website is not very user-friendly …*   *It's easy/difficult to navigate …*
> *It has a simple/complicated design …*   *The organization of the website is confusing …*

> The website has a cool design, but it's difficult to find …

> Having fewer icons on the page would make the website …

WRITING Writing a review

Write a short review of your cell phone. Describe what you like and don't like about it, and suggest how it can be improved.

> My cell phone is slim and light, but the screen is small. It's difficult to read the text when I'm typing because the keyboard is almost half the size of the screen. I would suggest …

Visitors testing the products on display at the Mobile World Congress in Barcelona

5 Community Builders

" ... news from Vila Cruzeiro often is not good news. But Vila Cruzeiro is also the place where our story begins. "

Dre Urhahn and Jeroen Koolhaas
Artists, TED speakers

UNIT GOALS

In this unit, you will ...

- talk about communities and ways to improve them.
- read about a unique way a college is educating communities.
- watch a TED Talk about how people can work together to transform their communities.

WARM UP

▶ **5.1** Watch part of Koolhaas and Urhahn's TED Talk. Answer the questions with a partner.

1 What do you know about Rio de Janeiro?

2 What do you think Vila Cruzeiro is like?

Volunteers and students painting a mural at a middle school in New York

5A Community building

VOCABULARY Making communities better

A Read the paragraph below. Then match each **bold** word to its definition.

Social **entrepreneurs** work to improve the lives of people and the **communities** they live in. Their businesses often focus on helping **underprivileged** people and communities. Sometimes, this involves **enhancing** or building **facilities** in the neighborhood, such as parks or schools. By creating jobs and improving environments, social entrepreneurs **empower** the underprivileged to make positive changes to their lives.

1 entrepreneurs   ○   ○ make someone stronger or more confident
2 communities   ○   ○ making something better
3 underprivileged ○   ○ groups of people living together in an area
4 enhancing   ○   ○ places or services provided for a particular purpose
5 facilities   ○   ○ people who start businesses
6 empower   ○   ○ without the opportunities of the average person

B Complete the sentences. Circle the correct words.

1 Elon Musk is a very successful (**community** / **entrepreneur**) who has started businesses in travel and space technology.

2 Medical (**facilities** / **entrepreneurs**) like hospices and hospitals are needed to support the elderly population.

3 A strong and stable economy can (**enhance** / **empower**) the quality of life for the average person.

4 Mother Teresa dedicated her life to helping the (**empowered** / **underprivileged**) in India.

C Work with a partner. What does your city or community do to help the underprivileged?

LISTENING Creating green spaces

> **Listening for intonation**
> Intonation helps you differentiate between questions and statements. Questions often end with a high intonation, while statements often end with a low intonation.

A ▶ **5.2** Watch social entrepreneur Martín Andrade talk about his foundation, Mi Parque. What is the aim of the foundation?

    a to reduce poverty and unemployment in Chile

    b to create more green parks for the underprivileged in Chile

B ▶ **5.3** Watch and check (✓) the things that the foundation does.

☐ It improves the housing conditions of low-income families.

☐ It educates the public about the importance of green spaces.

☐ It gets locals directly involved in planning and carrying out projects.

☐ It works with the government to get funding.

Martín Andrade with some local children in Chile

C **CRITICAL THINKING**

Evaluating In what ways does having green spaces benefit the people of an urban community? Discuss with a partner.

SPEAKING Talking about my community

A ▶ **5.4** What does Speaker B think her community needs?

A: Hey, I heard you just moved to a new neighborhood. How do you like it so far?

B: On the whole, I really like it. It's peaceful and there's a real sense of community. For example, there are often local events like weekend markets.

A: What about the local facilities? Are there many?

B: There are a few local shops and a supermarket.

A: Hmm. It sounds like a pretty nice area to live.

B: Yeah. I think it could certainly benefit from a sports complex, though. Right now, there's nowhere to play sports.

A: Well, where I live in the city is *too* noisy. And there are hardly any green spaces! We could really do with a park.

B Practice the conversation with a partner.

C Tell a partner about your community, and what you like or dislike about it. Use the expressions in blue above to help you.

> My community is really peaceful and quiet. I really like …

> I think my community could benefit from a movie theater. A lot of people in my neighborhood …

5B Changing places

LANGUAGE FOCUS Beautifying public spaces

A ▶ **5.5** Read the information. Do you know any places that have been transformed?

THE TRANSFORMATION OF MALACCA RIVER
SINCE 2002, THE MALACCA RIVER IN MALAYSIA HAS GONE THROUGH A HUGE TRANSFORMATION.

BEFORE  NOW

WHAT WAS DONE

 Pollution was removed from the river.

 The riverbank was strengthened with **concrete walls**.

 A **barrier** was constructed to prevent flooding.

 8 km of **walkways** were constructed on each side of the river.

 Riverside buildings were **repainted** with colorful murals.

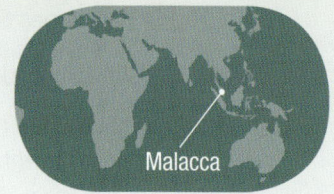 Malacca

B ▶ **5.6** Listen to the conversation. What impression does the woman have of Malacca? Discuss with a partner.

C ▶ **5.7** Watch and study the language in the chart.

Talking about how places have changed	
A construction company cleaned up the Malacca River. Architects transformed a church in Germany into a kindergarten.	The Malacca River was cleaned up. A church in Germany was transformed into a kindergarten.
A landscape architecture company designed the High Line Park in New York City. The Hong Kong government converted a landfill into a park.	The High Line Park in New York City was designed by a landscape architecture company. A landfill was converted into a park by the Hong Kong government.

For more information on **the passive**, see Grammar Summary 5 on page 185.

D ▶ **5.6** Listen to the conversation in **B** again. Complete the sentences from the conversation.

1 "But you wouldn't recognize it now. It's _____."

2 "It's all _____ . All the old buildings _____ into cool little shops and restaurants."

3 "And the buildings are brightly painted with murals that show Malacca's history and culture. They can _____ all along the river."

E Complete the sentences. Use the correct form of the words in parentheses.

1 The University of the Arts in London _____ (build) in 2008.

2 Air travel in Europe _____ (affect) after a volcano in Iceland erupted in 2010.

3 Mount Trashmore in the United States was a landfill that _____ (convert) into a park.

4 The Little Mermaid statue in Denmark _____ (damage) a number of times since the 1960s.

F ▶ **5.8** Complete the information. Circle the correct words. Then listen and check your answers.

Cheonggyecheon is a stream that flows through the middle of Seoul, South Korea. But the 11-kilometer stream is very different from how it ¹(**looked** / **has looked**) before—it ²(**is being transformed** / **has been transformed**) completely. Previously, the stream was covered by a large freeway. Then in 2003, the city government ³(**started** / **was started**) a huge project to restore it. The highway ⁴(**was removed** / **was being removed**), the stream ⁵(**is cleaned up** / **was cleaned up**), and the whole area was made into a park. Now, it ⁶(**is used** / **has been used**) by locals and tourists to relax and enjoy some greenery in the middle of the city.

Cheonggyecheon in Seoul, South Korea

SPEAKING Describing changes in my community

A How has your local community changed over time? Make a list of at least three ways in which it has changed.

B Create a simple timeline using the events you listed in **A**. Add details to each event.

C Work with a partner. Describe the changes in your community using your timeline. Give reasons for the changes and describe how you feel about them.

> A few months ago, a new train station was built near my house, so …

> My neighborhood wasn't really lively in the past, but recently a new shopping mall …

5C Barefoot College

PRE-READING Scanning

Scan the passage. Give an example of a skill that students learn at Barefoot College.

▶ 5.9

The Greek philosopher Aristotle once said, "For the things we have to learn before we can do them, we learn by doing them." This method of "learning by doing" has allowed Barefoot College to successfully train and educate millions of underprivileged people. Barefoot College was founded by Sanjit "Bunker" Roy. Shortly after graduating from Delhi University, Roy did some volunteer work in a poor region of India. The experience changed his life, and in 1972 he set up Barefoot College. His aim was to help rural[1] communities overcome their difficulties and become more independent.

Barefoot College is unlike any other college. All of its students around the world are from poor, rural communities. They don't have to be able to read or write—indeed, many can't. People of any age can attend—the school has a wide range of students, from children to grandmothers.

The college is owned and managed by everyone who works and learns there. These "Barefoot Professionals" are trained to perform all sorts of duties in the school, from providing dental[2] care services to cooking meals for staff and students.

No degrees or certificates are given out. But graduates return to their villages with their new skills and work to make their communities self-sufficient[3] by training other villagers. Being able to use their skills to serve their communities is **proof** of success.

The solar engineering program at Barefoot College has a **significant** role. Every year, the college **recruits** middle-aged women from rural villages that don't have electricity. For six months, the women learn how to build, install, use, and maintain solar lamps. The lack of a common language isn't a problem; they communicate through sign language and work with color-coded equipment. Through hands-on training, the women transform into solar engineers by the end of the program. The self-confidence they gain allows them to go on and inspire positive change in their villages. Since 2008, the women have managed to provide electricity to over 1,000 villages, bringing light to more than 40,000 households.

A student at Barefoot College builds a solar lamp.

Neema Gurung is one of the solar engineers at Barefoot College. With some financial help from the Indian government, she left her village in Nepal to take part in the program. As her village has no ⁵⁰ electricity, Gurung always had to finish her chores by sunset. For her, learning how to build solar lamps and bring light to her village will help greatly in **ensuring** the safety of her home. "Tigers often wander around our villages and have attacked ⁵⁵ locals in the past," Gurung explains. "It's like we are locked in our own house after darkness."

Barefoot College has demonstrated how education can empower rural people and help them live better lives. After its success in India, ⁶⁰ Barefoot College decided to expand its programs overseas. Today, it has a number of regional training centers in countries such as Ethiopia, Afghanistan, and Senegal. Through their hard work and **dedication**, thousands of ⁶⁵ Barefoot College graduates and teachers have transformed their communities into better places to live.

[1] **rural:** *adj.* of the countryside and not the city
[2] **dental:** *adj.* related to the teeth
[3] **self-sufficient:** *adj.* not requiring any form of help for survival

UNDERSTANDING MAIN IDEAS

Complete the profile of Barefoot College.

Barefoot College	
Founder	Sanjit "Bunker" Roy
Why was the college created?	While doing some ¹ _____ in a poor region of India, Roy was motivated to do something to help underprivileged communities.
Aim	The college was set up to help rural communities find solutions to their difficulties and become more ² _____ .
How is it different from most other colleges?	• Students don't need to be able to ³ _____ . • There is no ⁴ _____ limit. • No ⁵ _____ are given out after students complete their training.

UNDERSTANDING DETAILS

Complete the sentences about the solar engineering program. Circle the correct words.

1. The solar engineering program mainly trains (**young women** / **middle-aged women**).
2. To overcome the language differences among students, the college uses (**sign language** / **illustrations**) and color-coded equipment in its training.
3. After the training, the women (**educate people in their village** / **receive a job recommendation letter**).
4. Neema Gurung hopes to improve the (**accessibility** / **safety**) of her village after training at Barefoot College.

BUILDING VOCABULARY

A Complete the sentences with the words from the box.

proof	significant	recruit	ensuring	dedication

1. The success of Barefoot College is _____ that education can greatly improve the lives of rural people.
2. We need laws _____ that the rights of the underprivileged are protected.
3. The _____ of volunteers often inspires others to get involved.
4. Unlike most colleges, Barefoot College doesn't _____ students based on academic grades.
5. Barefoot College makes a(n) _____ difference to the lives of rural people by teaching them useful skills.

B CRITICAL THINKING

Reflecting Work with a partner. If you were able to interview Sanjit Roy to find out more about Barefoot College, what questions would you ask? Why?

5D How painting can transform communities

TEDTALKS

Artists **JEROEN KOOLHAAS** and **DRE URHAHN**—also known as Haas and Hahn—work on community projects in Rio de Janeiro. Seeing the **unfinished** buildings of the favelas—the crowded, **informal** neighborhoods of Rio de Janeiro—they worked with the locals to improve the community. Their **accomplishments** helped **transform** the favelas.

Haas and Hahn's idea worth spreading is that by bringing an entire community into the process of painting, neighborhoods can be transformed beautifully and residents benefit in ways far beyond what's visible.

PREVIEWING

Read the paragraphs above. Match each **bold** word to its meaning. You will hear these words in the TED Talk.

1 casual, not official   _____
2 incomplete   _____
3 successful achievements   _____
4 to change completely, usually for the better   _____

VIEWING

A ▶ **5.10** Watch Part 1 of the TED Talk. Answer questions 1 to 3.

1 Which of the following is true about Vila Cruzeiro?
    a It is located next to Copacabana Beach.
    b It was built largely by immigrants from Holland.
    c It is a community in the North Zone of Rio de Janeiro.

2 What surprised Haas and Hahn about the favelas?
    a Violent drug gangs live in the favelas.
    b The people who live in favelas are immigrants from the countryside.
    c The favelas were built without a master plan.

3 What made them want to start a painting project in the favelas?

   a The locals asked them to paint their houses.

   b They saw many unfinished houses.

   c They were inspired by some of the local artwork.

B ▶ **5.11** Watch Part 2 of the TED Talk. Order the events describing Haas and Hahn's first project from 1–6.

___1___ Haas and Hahn told a friend about their idea.

_____ They installed a kite on the hill.

_____ The locals hated it.

_____ They painted a house blue.

_____ They painted an image of a boy.

_____ News articles were written about their work.

C ▶ **5.12** Watch Part 3 of the TED Talk. Circle **T** for true or **F** for false.

1 Haas and Hahn were asked to transform North Philly through painting.   T   F

2 They organized and sent a team of designers from Holland to North Philly.   T   F

3 A different design was made for every house.   T   F

4 Local people were trained as painters for the project.   T   F

5 Haas and Hahn want to bring their idea to other countries.   T   F

D CRITICAL THINKING

Synthesizing/Reflecting Work with a partner. How is Haas and Hahn's approach to helping communities similar to Martín Andrade's (page 65)? Which of these projects would you like to do in your community? Why?

VOCABULARY IN CONTEXT

A ▶ **5.13** Watch the excerpts from the TED Talk. Choose the correct meaning of the words.

B Complete the sentences with the words from the box.

emerge	notorious	install	approach	bottom-up

1 Crowdfunding is one _____ to raising money for a good cause.

2 The favelas are _____ for problems like crime and poverty.

3 The favelas were built from the _____, without any master plan.

4 Sometimes, slums _____ when a large number of people from the countryside move to the city.

5 Haas and Hahn's first project in Rio de Janeiro was to create and _____ a piece of artwork in the favelas.

PRESENTATION SKILLS Ending with a hope for the future

One way to make the end of your presentation memorable is to close with a comment that expresses your hope for the future. This encourages the audience to reflect on your topic.

A ▶ 5.14 Watch part of Haas and Hahn's TED Talk. What expression do they use to end their presentation?

  a It's our dream that …

  b We hope … maybe one day …

  c We hope to see the world become …

B ▶ 5.15 Watch part of Kenneth Shinozuka's TED Talk. Complete the expression he uses to express his hope for the future.

"People living happily and healthily—that's _____."

Haas and Hahn's painting project in Santa Marta, Rio de Janeiro

5E Proposing changes

COMMUNICATE A neighborhood survey

A Work with two classmates. You are going to conduct a survey about their neighborhoods. Ask the questions below and make notes. Ask follow-up questions to get more information.

Questions	Neighborhood: _____	Neighborhood: _____
1 How would you describe your neighborhood?		
2 What facilities does your community have?		
3 Which facilities do you use?		
4 What kinds of events are organized locally?		
5 Is there a sense of community in your neighborhood? If yes, what gives it a sense of community?		
6 What kinds of improvements would you like to see in your neighborhood?		

B In your group, brainstorm specific ideas to improve the neighborhoods above.

> **Making suggestions**
> *It may be good to ...   Perhaps we could ...   Why don't we ...   One possible idea is ...*

> The neighborhood could do with more bicycle lanes for cyclists ...

> We could help underprivileged children in our neighborhood by donating books ...

WRITING Making a request

Write a short letter to your local government requesting a new feature, facility, or event for your neighborhood. Explain how it will help improve your community.

> I'm writing to suggest creating a community garden in our neighborhood. There are many nature lovers in our community, so it would be a good place for people to gather ...

A communal rooftop garden in Sydney, Australia

6 Clear Communication

"We desperately need great communication from our scientists and engineers."

Melissa Marshall
Communications teacher, TED speaker

UNIT GOALS

In this unit, you will …

- talk about methods of communication.
- read about powerful ways to get your ideas across.
- watch a TED Talk about how complex ideas can be made easy to understand.

WARM UP

▶ **6.1** Watch part of Melissa Marshall's TED Talk. Answer the questions with a partner.

1 Why is good communication from scientists and engineers so important?

2 Look through the unit. What types of communication methods and strategies do you see?

Two customers chatting in a café in Italy

6A Good communication

VOCABULARY Using communication collocations

A Cross out the phrase that doesn't belong in each group.

1	**have**	a meeting	~~a post~~	a conversation	5	**send**	an email	a meeting	a document
2	**give**	a text message	a report	a speech	6	**share**	a report	a comment	a phone call
3	**make**	a comment	a phone call	a letter	7	**write**	a meeting	a blog	a message
4	**post**	a letter	a text message	a comment	8	**check**	an email	a phone call	a message

B Work with a partner. Write one more example for each word below.

1 have _____
2 give _____
3 make _____
4 post _____

5 send _____
6 share _____
7 write _____
8 check _____

C Work with a partner. Choose the communication method you prefer. Tell your partner why you prefer it.

1 writing an email OR writing a letter
2 making a phone call OR sending a text message
3 giving a speech OR writing a report

LISTENING Communication styles

> **Describing styles and preferences**
> Listen for phrases that show what the speaker prefers to do.
> *Generally, I prefer to …   I usually try to …   I tend to …*

A ▶ **6.2** Watch author Neil Anderson talk about how he gives his presentations. Check (✓) the ways he prepares for them.

☐ He finds out about his audience.
☐ He calls teachers who are coming to his presentation.
☐ He makes sure he knows his presentation topic well.
☐ He prepares a list of useful reference materials.
☐ He creates slides.

B ▶ **6.2** Watch again. How does Anderson make his audience feel more involved in his presentations? Discuss with a partner.

Neil Anderson speaking to a group of teachers

C **CRITICAL THINKING**

Reflecting Work with a partner. Which of Anderson's methods would you use if you gave a presentation? Why?

SPEAKING Talking about communication preferences

A ▶ **6.3** If you need to get in touch with Speaker B, what is the best way to contact him?

A: Hey, did you see the message I sent you on Facebook yesterday?

B: Sorry, I don't often log in to check my Facebook account—I prefer talking on the phone. Was it something urgent?

A: Oh, not really. I just wanted to ask you to upload the photos from the party the other day.

B: Oh, sure. I'll do that tomorrow after I'm done working on my presentation.

A: Thanks. Is the presentation for that science project you mentioned?

B: Yeah, it is. So I'll probably be pretty busy today. You should call if you need me.

A: OK. Good luck with your presentation!

B Practice the conversation with a partner.

C Work with a partner. Talk about the communication methods or tools you frequently use. Use the expressions in blue above to help you.

> How often do you check your Facebook account?
>
> Not very often. I prefer texting. What about you?
>
> I log in to Facebook every day. I use it to …

6B How do you communicate?

LANGUAGE FOCUS Describing types of communicators

A ▶ **6.4** Read about the four types of communicators below. Which do you think you are? Look at the flowchart on page 171 and find out.

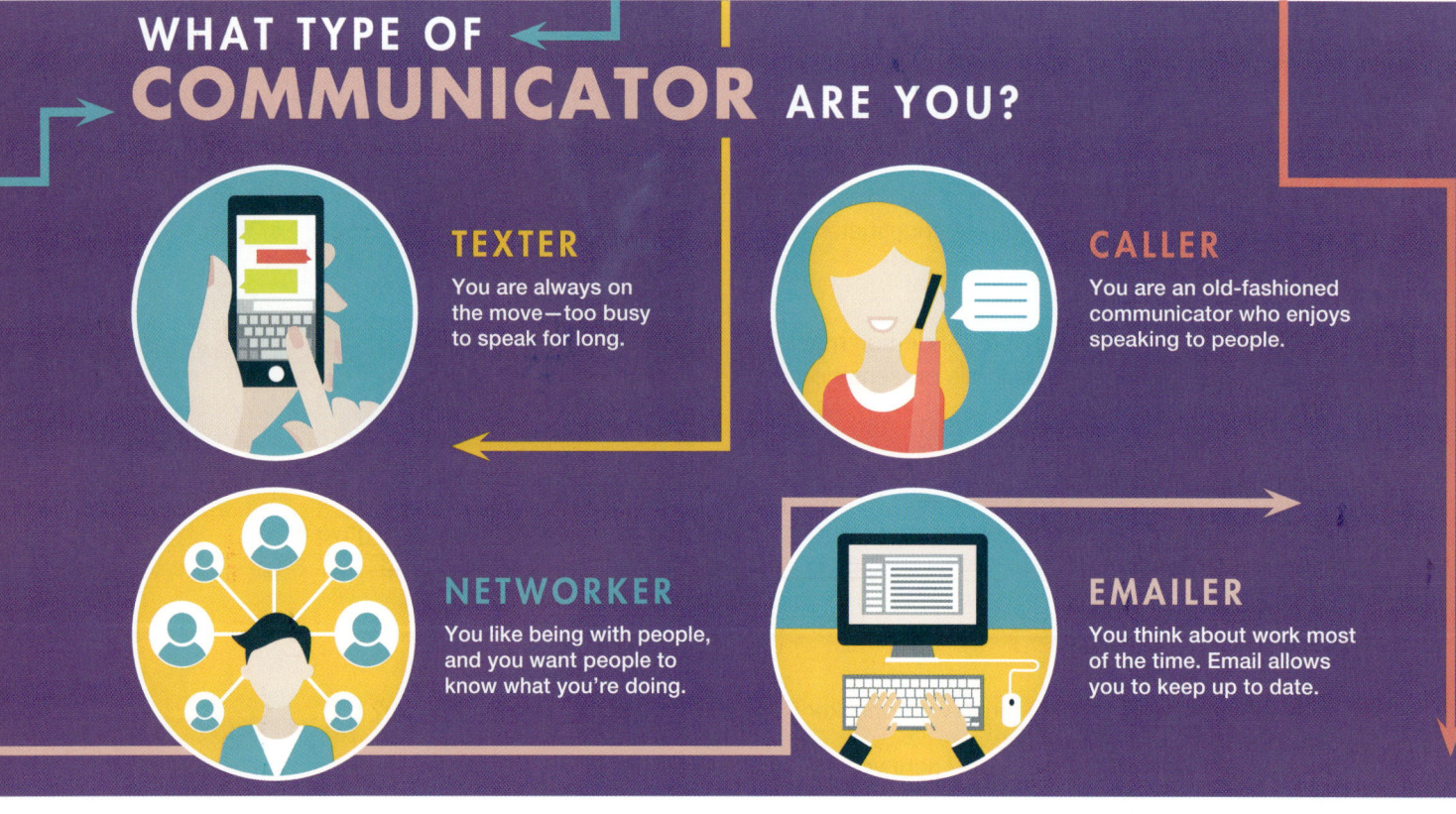

B ▶ **6.5** Listen to the conversation. What kind of communicators described in **A** do you think the two speakers are?

Jon: _____   Mel: _____

C ▶ **6.6** Watch and study the language in the chart.

Talking about communication preferences	
I generally	avoid texting people. hate calling people. recommend posting a comment online.
She	tries to call her parents every week. prefers to use social media to connect with people. promised to send a postcard.
Social networking allows me to keep in touch with my friends. I don't like my friends to text me. Video calling helps me (to) stay in touch with my family.	

For more information on **verb patterns with -ing and infinitive**, see Grammar Summary 6 on pages 185–186.

D ▶ **6.5** Listen to the conversation in **B** again. Complete the sentences from the conversation.

1 "I much prefer _____ to people."

2 "I usually _____ because people are always busy and they never answer."

E Find and correct the mistake in each sentence. Do you agree with the statements? Tell a partner the reasons for your answers.

1 It may be stressful, but we should all learn how to speaking in public.

2 I think that use social media is a waste of time.

3 The government should try to persuade people being polite online.

4 I prefer to emailing over talking on the phone.

5 To text encourages us to be lazy writers.

6 It's better to call someone than text them when you want asking for help.

F ▶ **6.7** Complete the information. Circle the correct words. Then listen and check your answers.

Many people worry that ¹(**to text** / **texting**) will make people ²(**to forget** / **forget**) how to write well. This isn't a new concern. Throughout history, people have always complained about young people ³(**to use** / **using**) incorrect grammar. In fact, more than 2,000 years ago, there were already complaints about people ⁴(**using** / **use**) bad Latin! Some language experts believe that texting is actually a new kind of language—it allows us ⁵(**to write** / **write**) more like the way we speak.

Texting is one of the main modes of communication for many teens today.

SPEAKING Communication methods

Work with a partner. What methods of communication do you think are most appropriate for the situations below? Why?

1 Two of your friends are getting married. You'd like to congratulate them.

2 You need to apologize to a customer for sending the wrong information.

3 You have to tell your employees that they are going to lose their jobs because the office is closing.

4 You are not happy in your current relationship. You have decided you are going to break it off.

> I think the best way to congratulate my friends would be to send them a card because …

> I think it's better to call them because …

6C Communication in the digital age

PRE-READING Reflecting

Work with a partner. Have you seen or heard a speech recently that you really enjoyed? What did you like most about it?

▶ 6.8

We live in an age of information overload.[1] Research shows that the average social media user receives about 300 pieces of content a day—roughly equivalent to the number of words in a standard novel. With such a huge amount of content available, people are likely to spend less time going through each piece of information. Therefore, data has to be delivered quickly and effectively in order to grab people's attention.

SEVEN WAYS TO COMMUNICATE MORE EFFECTIVELY

Here are some suggestions on ways we can engage our audience in our writing and during presentations:

Use subheadings. They allow you to group your ideas and guide your readers.

Describe your ideas in a simple way. To test whether your description is simple enough, try explaining it to someone who knows nothing about your topic. But make sure that you keep the essential parts—avoid dumbing ideas down until they lose their meaning.

Present ideas logically and concisely. Use clear language and avoid technical words.

Include stories. Personal stories can provide a human connection and make your point more memorable.

Give analogies. They help to make complex ideas meaningful. For example, you could describe electricity as water flowing through a pipe.

ONLINE STRATEGIES

According to a 2015 study by Microsoft, the average Internet user is estimated to have an attention **span** of about eight seconds—even shorter than that of a goldfish! Other research also shows that one in three users will switch websites if the page doesn't load within five seconds. So how can writers keep online readers' attention and interest? Below are a few things to note for online communication:

- **Highlight your main goal right at the start**—grab the viewer's attention immediately with a short and clear message.
- **Use bullet points** to reduce the amount of text and focus attention on the most important details.
- **Ensure that pages load fast.** There are many web resources that can analyze websites and suggest ways to make them faster.
- **Avoid cluttering[2] the page**—less is definitely more when it comes to web design.

9 seconds attention span of a goldfish

8 seconds attention span of an Internet user

80

A commuter reading on her phone on a crowded train in Hong Kong

30 **Use quotes.** They are often interesting ways to start or end a presentation, and can be a source of humor.

Use attractive visuals. Visual aids such as photographs, diagrams, and charts can appeal 35 directly to your audience's imagination and create a more **lasting** impact.

GETTING OUR IDEAS ACROSS

Gone are the days when only a select few could share their ideas with a wide audience. Today, 40 modern technology allows anyone to reach a wide audience. Now that we have this power, it is even more important that we learn to present our thoughts clearly and effectively in the digital age.

[1] **overload:** *n.* too much of something
[2] **clutter:** *v.* to fill something in a messy way

UNDERSTANDING MAIN IDEAS

What is the main purpose of the passage?

a to explain how technology helps us communicate

b to suggest ways to increase people's attention span

c to discuss how we can get our ideas across effectively

UNDERSTANDING DETAILS

A Choose the correct options.

1 The Online Strategies section gives data on our attention spans to show that _____.

   a people have become slower at reading

   b websites need to engage readers very quickly

   c more people prefer to get information online

2 Which of the following is the author likely to agree with?

   a Social media sites are becoming reliable sources of information.

   b Online content writers tend to focus more on text than design.

   c With access to technology, people can now reach out to a very wide audience.

B Match the sentences to the communication tips that they illustrate.

1 Look at the Venn diagram on the screen. ○   ○ Include stories.

2 This reminds me of a challenge I faced in my youth. ○   ○ Give analogies.

3 The human liver is like a chemical factory. ○   ○ Use quotes.

4 As John F. Kennedy once said, "Ask not what your country ○   ○ Use attractive
   can do for you, ask what you can do for your country."   visuals.

BUILDING VOCABULARY

A Complete the sentences using the correct form of the words in blue from the passage.

1 The average human life _____ has increased greatly over the last 100 years.

2 Learning how to write _____ is one of the most important skills for a writer.

3 Don't complicate your essay with too many _____ terms.

4 The treatment had a(n) _____ effect on me—I no longer get backaches.

5 Comparing the human brain to a computer can be a good _____ for describing how the brain works.

B CRITICAL THINKING

Evaluating Look at the passage again. Choose three ideas for effective communication that you think are important. Explain your choices to a partner.

6D Talk nerdy to me

TEDTALKS

MELISSA MARSHALL works at the Department of Communication Arts & Sciences at Penn State University. She specializes in teaching speaking skills to engineering students.

Melissa Marshall's idea worth spreading is that even complex and technical topics can be easy to understand and exciting if they are communicated in the right ways.

PREVIEWING

Read the paragraph below. Match each **bold** word to its meaning. You will hear these words in the TED Talk.

Melissa Marshall believes that we **desperately** need great communication from our scientists and engineers. This is because scientists **tackle** some of the world's biggest problems—like climate change. While it is important for scientists to make everyone understand their work, Marshall points out that they must not **dumb down** their ideas. Scientists need to communicate their ideas without **compromising** them. Marshall also recommends that scientists use stories to **engage** us and get us excited.

1 making something weaker   _____
2 to make something too simple   _____
3 to form a connection with   _____
4 seriously; urgently   _____
5 to deal with (a problem)   _____

VIEWING

A ▶ **6.9** Watch Part 1 of the TED Talk. Choose the correct options.

1 What analogy does Marshall use?
   a an animal
   b a fantasy story

2 Why do you think she makes this analogy?
   a to describe how unfamiliar the situation was for her
   b to describe how exciting the situation was

3 What is the amazing new world that Marshall wants us to see?
   a the ideas that scientists and engineers have
   b the lives of scientists and engineers

B ▶ **6.10** Watch Part 2 of the TED Talk. Check (✓) the advice that Marshall has for scientists and engineers.

☐ Show how science is relevant to non-scientists.
☐ Give demonstrations where possible.
☐ Avoid using jargon when speaking.
☐ Simplify ideas as much as possible.
☐ Don't use bullet points in presentations.
☐ Use less text and more visuals on slides.

C ▶ **6.11** Watch Part 3 of the TED Talk. Discuss these questions with a partner.

1 Why do you think Marshall uses an equation to summarize her talk? What do you think it means?
2 Can you think of another technique she could have used to end her presentation in a memorable way?

D CRITICAL THINKING

Evaluating/Synthesizing Discuss these questions with a partner.

1 Look at the photo at the bottom of the page. Do you like it? How effective do you think it is as a way of communicating information?
2 Compare Marshall's recommendations with the advice in the reading on pages 80–81. How similar are they?

An infographic on a Kulula Airlines plane

VOCABULARY IN CONTEXT

A ▶ **6.12** Watch the excerpts from the TED Talk. Choose the correct meaning of the words.

B Complete the sentences using the words in the box.

| beware of | barriers to | key into | by all means |

1 Keep your presentation slides simple to allow the audience to _____ the main point on each slide.

2 When making online purchases, you need to _____ hidden costs.

3 Language differences are not necessarily _____ intercultural understanding—we can learn about other cultures through music, food, or art.

4 If you feel confident, _____ apply for the job.

PRESENTATION SKILLS Engaging with your audience

> Make your presentation seem like a conversation in order to connect with your audience. Here are some ways you can do this:
> - Make eye contact.
> - Use relaxed and friendly body language.
> - Talk enthusiastically—let your personality come through.

A ▶ **6.13** Watch part of Melissa Marshall's TED Talk. Check (✓) the techniques that she uses.

Melissa Marshall _____.
- ☐ speaks energetically
- ☐ asks the audience questions
- ☐ smiles and uses humor
- ☐ gets someone to join her onstage
- ☐ is relaxed while presenting
- ☐ checks her audience's understanding before continuing

B Work with a partner. What advantages are there to making a presentation like a conversation?

> I think a presentation that feels like a conversation allows the audience to relax while listening.

C Work in groups. Brainstorm other ways to make a presentation feel like a conversation.

6E Simplifying ideas

COMMUNICATE Explaining a topic of interest

A You are going to explain a particular idea or concept. It can be a game, a sport, a hobby, or an idea from your work or study. Choose a topic and write some notes on it below.

> My topic:
>
> Key points:

B Decide how you will explain the topic. Think about how you can make it easy to understand.

> **Giving an explanation**
> I'd like to tell you more about … … is like a(n) …
> The basic idea of … is … You can think of it as a(n) …

C Work in groups. Take turns explaining your topic to your group members.

WRITING Giving an explanation

Choose one of the topics that your group members talked about. Write a paragraph about what it is and what you learned about it.

> One of my group members talked about ice hockey. It's a sport that's popular in parts of North America and Europe. There are six players on each team, including one goaltender. The aim is to score more points than the other team by …

A player scores in an ice hockey match.

Presentation 2

MODEL PRESENTATION

A Complete the transcript of the presentation using the words in the box.

| better | to share | upload | submit |
| app | are fixed | more efficient | most important |

Hi, I'm Scott. It's great to be here today. Tell me, how many of you have noticed a problem in your neighborhood, like broken street lights? Right, most of you. And how many of you reported it to the local government? Hmm, nobody. Today, I'm going to explain a simple idea that can help people improve their neighborhood.

My idea is for an ^{1}_____, which allows you ^{2}_____ and report local issues. Imagine you're walking down the street and you find a tree blocking the way or trash dumped in a park. You take some photos and open up the app. You ^{3}_____ the photo and add any comments you want. Everyone can then see the details on a map. You can see the issues that people report and when they ^{4}_____. Here, you can see the photo of the problem and the location on the map. And here is a list of things that people can ^{5}_____. But that's not all. Users can vote on the ^{6}_____ issues and which should be fixed first. So we all help to improve the local area as well as make the government ^{7}_____.

So, that's my idea for how we can all help make our neighborhoods ^{8}_____. Actually, there are some cities around the world doing this already. My hope is that the idea will spread to all our neighborhoods, so we can all enjoy a more pleasant and safe environment. Thank you for listening.

B ▶ **P.2** Watch the presentation and check your answers.

C ▶ **P.2** Review the list of presentation skills from Units 1–6 below. Which does the speaker use? Check (✓) them as you watch again. Then compare with a partner.

The speaker …
- helps the audience visualize by
   - doing a demonstration ☐
   - giving interesting facts ☐
   - telling a story ☐
   - using visuals ☐
- comments on visuals ☐
- opens with an interesting fact ☐
- asks the audience questions ☐
- ends with a hope for the future ☐
- engages with the audience ☐

YOUR TURN

A You are going to plan and give a short presentation to explain an idea for improving communication among residents and strengthening the local sense of community. Think about how you could use technology to help the community connect with each other. Make notes in the chart below.

How do people in your neighborhood communicate with one another now?

How close are people in your neighborhood?

How can technology help to improve communication?

B Look at the useful phrases in the box below. Think about which ones you will need in your presentation.

> **Useful phrases**
>
> **Asking the audience questions:** *What do you think of when …?*
> *How many of you …?*
>
> **Making suggestions:** *My idea is for a/an … that …*
> *What I'd like to propose is …*
> *One way to improve communication is …*
>
> **Describing communities:** *tight-knit, supportive, united*

C Work with a partner. Take turns giving your presentation using your notes. Use some of the presentation skills from Units 1–6 below. As you listen, check (✓) each skill your partner uses.

> The speaker …
> - helps the audience visualize by
>   - doing a demonstration ☐
>   - giving interesting facts ☐
>   - telling a story ☐
>   - using visuals ☐
> - comments on visuals ☐
> - opens with an interesting fact ☐
> - asks the audience questions ☐
> - ends with a hope for the future ☐
> - engages with the audience ☐

D Give your partner some feedback on their talk. Include at least two things you liked and one thing that could be improved.

> I liked your presentation. You asked questions and shared an interesting story. But the end of your talk was a bit abrupt.

7 Identity

" Where do you come from? It's such a simple question, but these days, of course, simple questions bring ever more complicated answers. "

Pico Iyer
Travel writer, TED speaker

UNIT GOALS

In this unit, you will …

- talk about factors that influence people's sense of identity.
- read about different types of migration.
- watch a TED Talk about the meaning of "home."

WARM UP

▶ **7.1** Watch part of Pico Iyer's TED Talk. Answer the questions with a partner.

1 Why is it hard for Pico Iyer to answer the question about where he is from?

2 How would you answer the question in the quote? Is your answer different depending on who is asking?

89

Soccer fans celebrate Germany's victory at the 2014 World Cup.

7A Where are you from?

VOCABULARY Describing identity

A ▶ **7.2** Complete the sentences using the words from the box. Then listen and check your answers.

| sense of identity | multicultural | background | factors |
| traditional | migrants | have a lot in common | |

1 A person's _____ is how they see themselves, and it usually depends on many different _____ .

2 Even if two people are from different countries, they may still _____ .

3 The United States has a _____ society, consisting of people from different ethnic groups.

4 Every year, millions of _____ move to other countries for work or to find better lives.

5 In today's globalized world, the _____ idea that people are mainly from a monocultural _____ is becoming less true.

B Work with a partner. Discuss these questions.

1 How multicultural is your country? Which cultures are the most common?
2 What are some traditional cultural practices in your country?

> My country is very multicultural. There are …

> Most of the people in my country are Vietnamese. But we have a growing group of …

LISTENING Multicultural experiences

> **Listening for opinions**
> You can identify the speaker's opinions by listening for phrases that introduce thoughts.
> *I would say that …*   *To me, …*   *I think the best part is …*

A ▶ **7.3** Watch Janice Reis Lodge talk about her background. Match the parts of the sentences to complete the descriptions about her life and family.

1 She was born in   ○   ○ Singapore.
2 She met her husband in   ○   ○ the United Kingdom.
3 Her husband is from   ○   ○ South Africa.
4 Her children were born in ○   ○ Portugal.
5 She now lives in   ○   ○ Hong Kong.

B ▶ **7.4** Watch Reis Lodge talk about her sense of home and identity. What does "home" mean to her? Discuss with a partner.

C CRITICAL THINKING

Reflecting Work with a partner. What does Reis Lodge and her family enjoy about being able to experience various cultures?

Janice Reis Lodge with her children

SPEAKING Talking about your background

A ▶ **7.5** What does Speaker B plan to do next year?

A: You've been living here for a couple of years now, right?
B: Yeah, it's a wonderful place. And the people are really friendly.
A: Glad you like it. Do you plan to stay in Argentina for a while longer?
B: Actually, I'll probably move to Thailand next year.
A: Oh, is that where you're from?
B: My mother's Thai, but I grew up in France. My dad was working there. He's American.
A: Wow! I've never lived overseas. I've lived here all my life.
B: Really? Would you like to live abroad for a while?
A: I'm not sure. All my family and friends are here.

B Practice the conversation with a partner.

C Work with a partner. Write three things about your background that most people don't know. Then share them with your partner. Use the expressions in blue above to help you.

_____   _____   _____

> I lived in Canada for two years.

> My great-grandparents are from Brazil, but my parents grew up in Japan.

7B Global movement

LANGUAGE FOCUS Discussing human migration

A ▶ 7.6 Look at the information. What could be some reasons for the differences between migration patterns in 1990 and 2013?

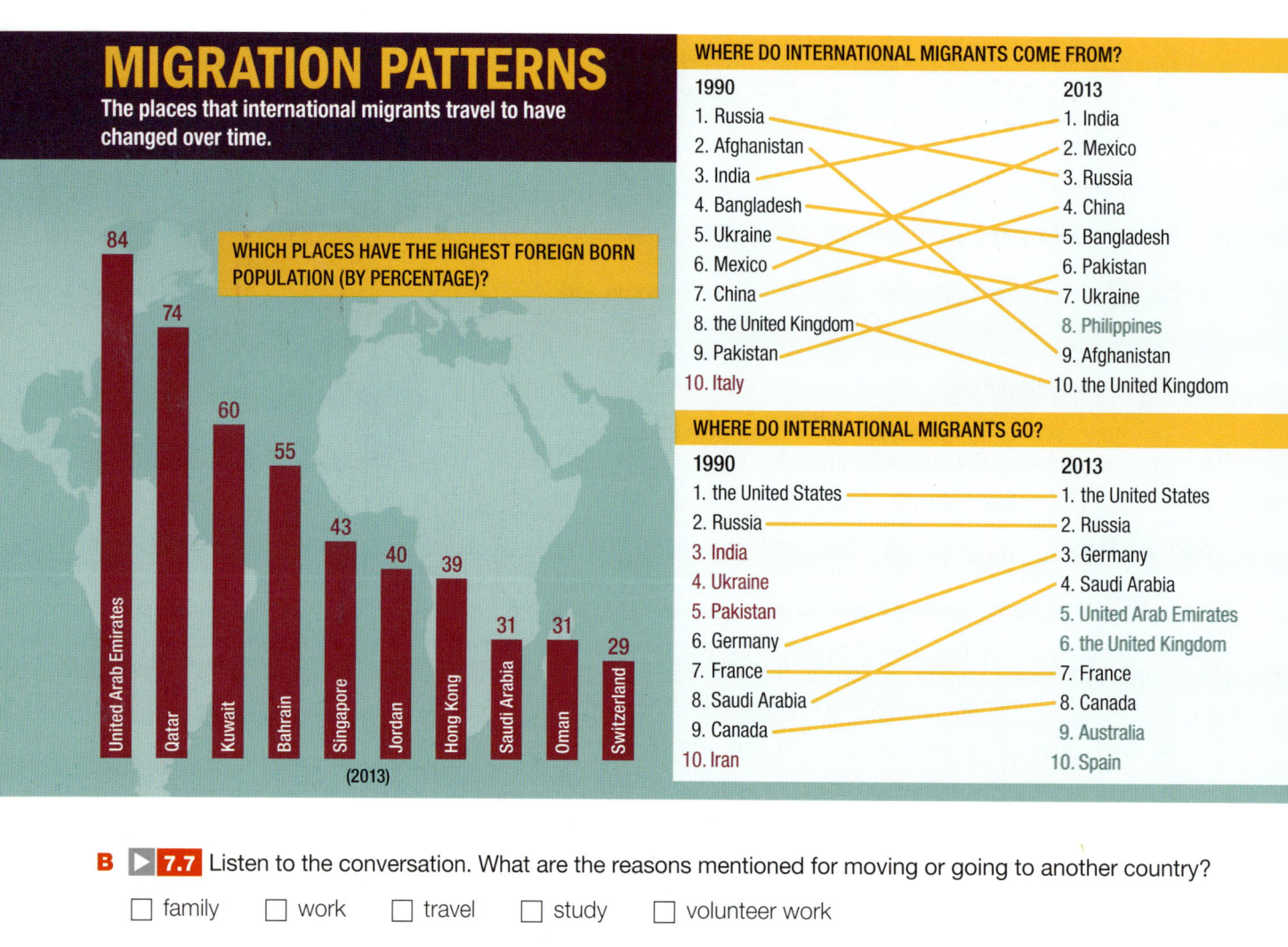

B ▶ 7.7 Listen to the conversation. What are the reasons mentioned for moving or going to another country?

☐ family   ☐ work   ☐ travel   ☐ study   ☐ volunteer work

C ▶ 7.8 Watch and study the language in the chart.

Talking about ongoing actions and events
I've been living in France since 2015. The number of people moving to the United States has been increasing.
The economy hasn't been doing well this year. I haven't been keeping up to date with the latest technological trends.
How long have you been studying overseas? / I've been studying overseas for three years. Have you been working at your company for long? / Yes, I have. / No, I haven't.

For more information on the **present perfect progressive**, see Grammar Summary 7 on page 187.

D ▶ **7.7** Listen to the conversation in **B** again. Circle **T** for true or **F** for false.

1. The woman's colleague has been living in France.   T F
2. The man's sister has been working at her current company for five years.   T F
3. The man has lived in the same country all his life.   T F

E ▶ **7.9** Complete the conversation. Circle the correct words. Then listen and check your answers.

A: Hi! It's been a while. How have you been?

B: Good. Actually, ¹(**I got** / **I've been getting**) ready to go overseas. I leave next week.

A: Really? Where are you going?

B: New Zealand. I've never been there before. ²(**I've been** / **I'm**) looking forward to going for ages.

A: How long will you be there?

B: Six months. ³(**I'll be** / **I've been**) studying and also traveling around the country.

A: Wow, sounds great. Actually, ⁴(**I'm** / **I've been**) reading about New Zealand recently. It sounds like a great place to visit.

B: Yeah. There are a lot of fun things to do. I've checked them out on the Internet. So what about you? Are you planning any trips?

A: Not right now. ⁵(**I'm** / **I've been**) pretty busy at work these past few months.

The number of people visiting New Zealand has been increasing; more than 3 million people visited in 2015.

SPEAKING Talking about living abroad

Find a person for each of the items in the chart. It could also be someone your classmate knows. Write their names and ask a follow-up question to get more information.

Find someone who …	Name	Details
has been living in this city for more than ten years.		
has family or friends in at least two other countries.		
comes from a different city or country.		
would like to move to a different city or country in the future.		
has been studying English for more than five years.		

Have you been living in Rio de Janeiro for more than ten years?

No, I only moved here six years ago.

7C Global migration

PRE-READING Predicting

Work with a partner. What do you think are some of the reasons people decide to move to a different region or country?

▶ 7.10

1   We live in an **era** of globalization; about 250 million people worldwide now live in countries other than the one in which they were born. This constant movement of people
5   complicates a question that used to be so much simpler: "Where are you from?"

People move countries for a **diverse** range of reasons. Economic migrants look overseas for better work opportunities and an improved standard of
10 living. They often travel to one of the many developed countries. These countries often have low birthrates, and as a result, are in need of working-age adults. Globalization has led to the overseas expansion of many businesses, allowing skilled workers to take up
15 jobs outside of their home countries.

Then there are retirees[1]—people who want to spend their later years in a country with a lower cost of living. This group of migrants usually comes from countries where the cost of retirement is expensive.

20 These first two groups of people move to countries of their own choice, but a third group is not so lucky. Refugees are migrants who are forced to leave their homes for reasons such as **conflict** in their countries. These migrants often have to **undertake**
25 dangerous journeys in order to escape.

The distribution of migrants around the world is not even. Today, the United Arab Emirates (UAE) is one of the top destinations for economic migrants: they make up over 80 percent of the population.
30 In Asia, the distribution varies greatly: About four in ten people living in Hong Kong are foreign-born, but Japan's migrant population is just one in fifty. Where migrants go depends on many factors, such as job opportunities or cultural and language differences.

35 A large-scale **influx** of migrants can create tensions within the host country, and it is sometimes perceived that migrants create a drain[2] on that country's resources. This is a controversial point, however, and many people disagree. A study by
40 researchers Christian Dustmann and Tommaso Frattini showed that on the whole, migrants from Europe contributed more to Britain's economy than they benefited from the value of public services.

Migrants also help support the economy of
45 their home countries. Most send money home

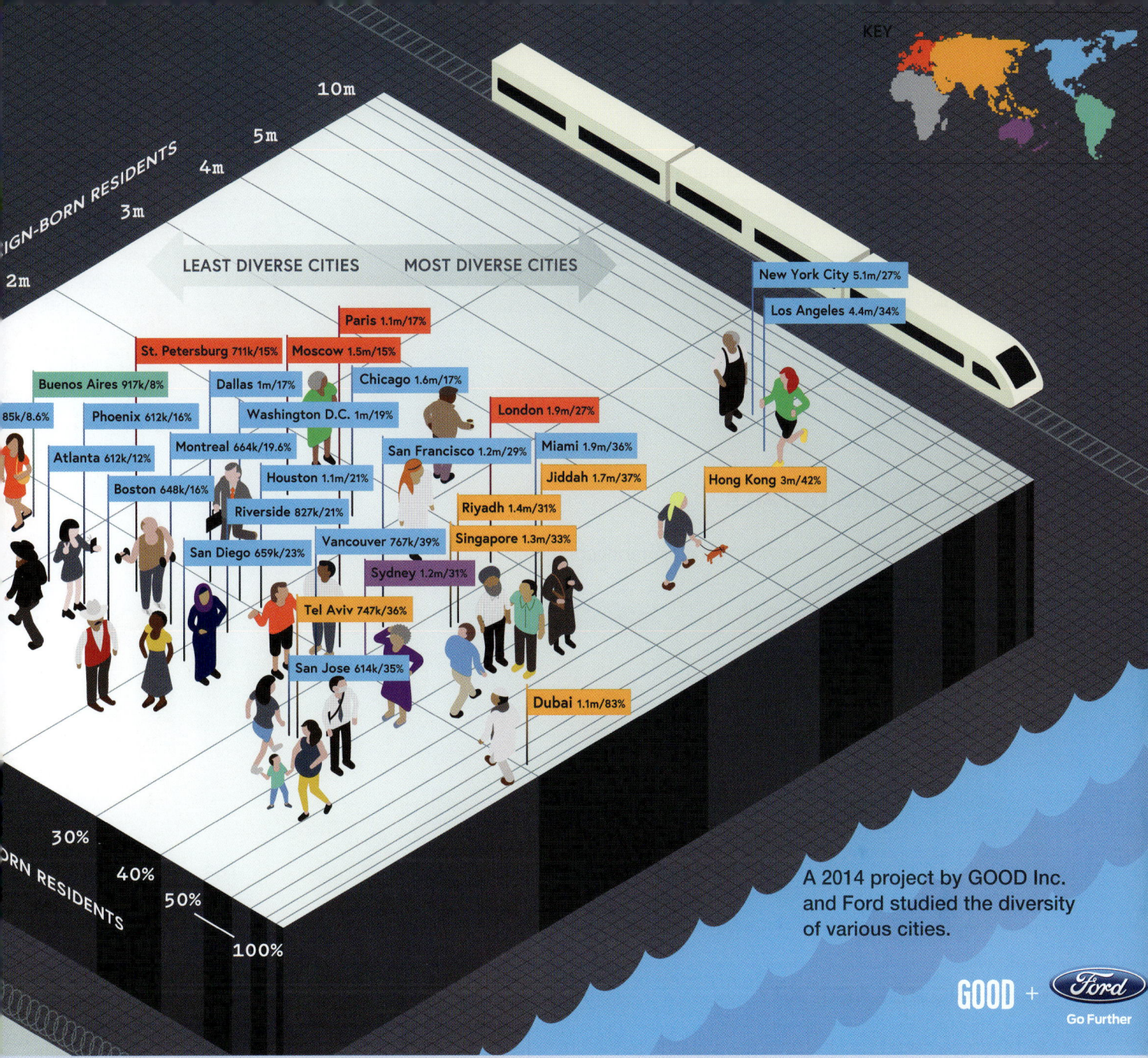

A 2014 project by GOOD Inc. and Ford studied the diversity of various cities.

to their families; the World Bank estimates that international migrants sent home about $600 billion in 2015, an amount comparable to the national wealth of the twentieth richest country in the world.

In addition to the economic benefits, migrants may contribute to the cultural diversity of their host countries. The International Organization for Migration (IOM), for example, believes the movement of people around the world to be a positive force. It works with governments to protect migrants' rights. Through a global campaign called "Migrants Contribute," it also raises awareness of the value of migrants' contributions.

As we move toward an increasingly multicultural world, we can observe how a blend of cultures creates **vibrancy** in different countries. Being able to experience multiple cultures just by walking down the street is something that our grandparents might never have imagined. In many global cities today, it's already a reality.

[1] **retirees:** *n.* people who have stopped working because they no longer need to

[2] **drain:** *n.* something that uses up time, money, etc.

SUMMARIZING KEY POINTS

Complete the chart about global migration.

Global Migration	
Types of migrants	Reasons for migrating
1 Economic migrants	
2	
3	

UNDERSTANDING DETAILS

Complete the concept map showing how migrants contribute in different ways.

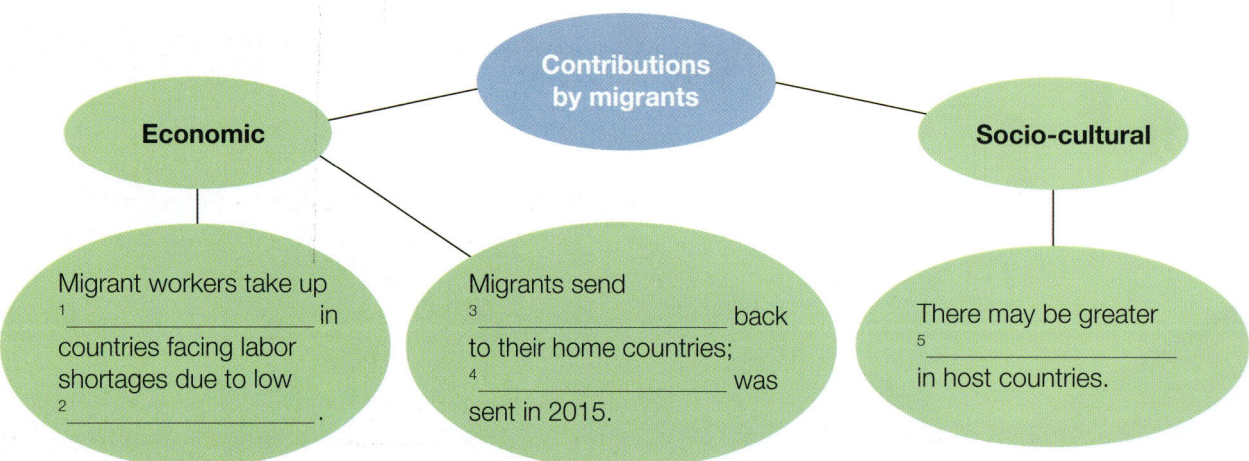

Contributions by migrants

Economic

Socio-cultural

Migrant workers take up ¹_____ in countries facing labor shortages due to low ²_____.

Migrants send ³_____ back to their home countries; ⁴_____ was sent in 2015.

There may be greater ⁵_____ in host countries.

BUILDING VOCABULARY

A Match the words in blue from the passage to their definitions.

1 conflict   ○   ○ try to do something

2 undertake ○   ○ the arrival of a large number of people

3 influx   ○   ○ fighting between groups of people

B Complete the information using the words in blue from the passage.

We live in a(n) ¹_____ of global movement and travel. Well-connected air, land, and sea routes allow people to go anywhere they wish. With all this movement and interaction of people all over the world, we are able to experience a(n) ²_____ range of cultures and customs. The presence of people from different backgrounds living together creates a(n) ³_____ and an energy that bring the world closer.

C CRITICAL THINKING

Inferring Work with a partner. What attitude does the author of the article have toward global migration? Do you think some people might have an opinion of migration that is different from the author's? Why?

7D Where is home?

TEDTALKS

PICO IYER has traveled widely throughout the world and is best known for his travel writing. He explores the meaning of "home," what it means to be on your own, the joy of travel, and how travel can help us focus in a world of technological distractions.

Pico Iyer's idea worth spreading is that our "home" is not just the place where we are born and raised; it's the place where we feel we have truly become ourselves.

PREVIEWING

Read the paragraph below. Match each **bold** word to its meaning. You will hear these words in the TED Talk.

More and more people now live in a different country than the one in which they grew up. In the past, most people probably felt somewhat **alien** whenever they traveled outside their own country. It may also have been less common for locals to see or interact with **foreigners** in their countries. But the situation is different now. The traditional idea of people having single cultural backgrounds is slowly **evolving**. People with multicultural backgrounds now **represent** a new normal: a mix of languages, **ancestry**, cultures, and customs.

1 be an example of   _____
2 changing   _____
3 your family's history   _____
4 people from a country other than yours   _____
5 strange or unfamiliar   _____

VIEWING

A ▶ **7.11** Watch Part 1 of the TED Talk. Why could Pico Iyer be considered as these nationalities? Match the nationalities to the reasons.

Pico Iyer could be considered …

1 Indian   ○   ○ because it is his birthplace and where he grew up.
2 English   ○   ○ because it is where his ancestors were from.
3 American   ○   ○ because he likes the place and spends a lot of time there.
4 Japanese   ○   ○ because it is where he pays his taxes and sees his doctor.

B Work with a partner. Pico Iyer says that he doesn't really belong to any of the nationalities in **A**. What reasons does he give?

C ▶ 7.12 Watch Part 2 of the TED Talk. Pico Iyer describes the "floating tribe" (people who live in countries not their own) in two ways. Check (✓) the diagrams that best illustrate what he says.

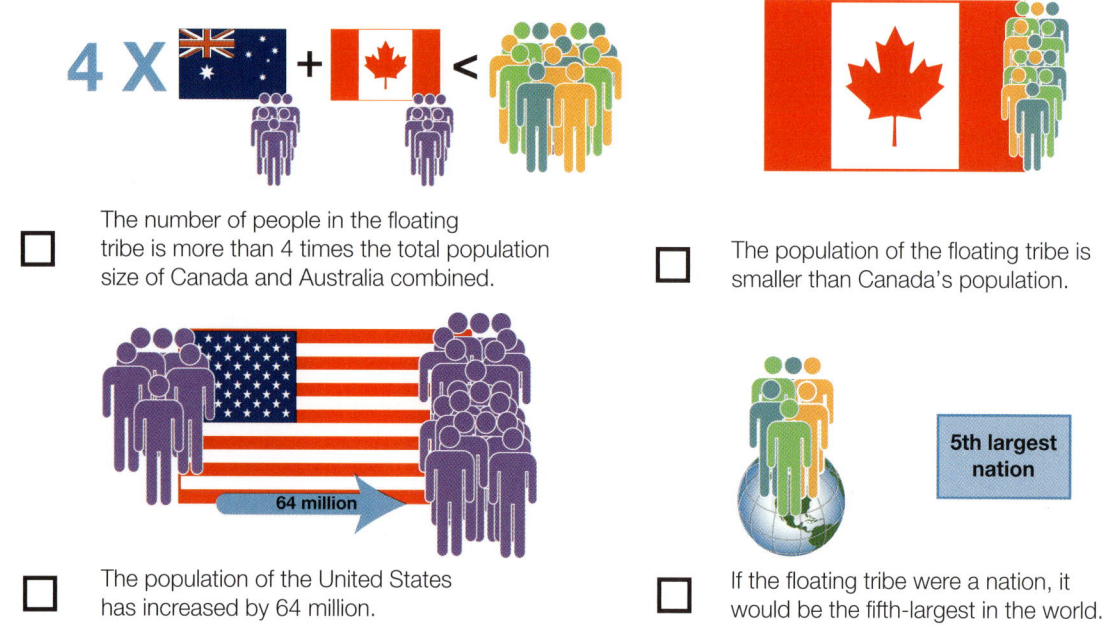

☐ The number of people in the floating tribe is more than 4 times the total population size of Canada and Australia combined.

☐ The population of the floating tribe is smaller than Canada's population.

☐ The population of the United States has increased by 64 million.

☐ If the floating tribe were a nation, it would be the fifth-largest in the world.

D ▶ 7.13 Watch Part 3 of the TED Talk. Discuss these questions with a partner.

1 What is Pico Iyer's attitude toward the people belonging to the floating tribe? Give examples from his talk to explain your answer.

2 Why does Pico Iyer think the young man and the young woman he describes in his talk probably have a lot in common?

E **CRITICAL THINKING**

Synthesizing Work with a partner. How do Pico Iyer's opinions compare with the author's opinions on pages 94–95? Do they have anything in common?

VOCABULARY IN CONTEXT

A ▶ 7.14 Watch the excerpts from the TED Talk. Choose the correct meaning of the words.

B Complete the sentences using the expressions in the box. Two are extra.

| earned the right to | tribe | unimaginable | exhilarating | blend of |

1 New York City is a diverse place with a(n) _____ ethnicities.

2 The Internet has resulted in new methods of learning and communication that were previously _____ .

3 Visiting culturally diverse places can lead to _____ new experiences.

PRESENTATION SKILLS Using stories to personalize your message

> Stories are powerful ways to personalize your message and illustrate your points. You can use both real and fictional stories.

A ▶ **7.15** Watch part of Pico Iyer's TED Talk. Why does he tell this story?

  a to describe the people he was close to

  b to show how different he felt from his classmates

  c to explain why he wanted to be different from his classmates

B Match the TED speakers below to the stories that they told.

  1 Kenneth Shinozuka ○   ○ teaching a class of engineering students

  2 Haas and Hahn ○   ○ seeing a family member wander around at night

  3 Melissa Marshall ○   ○ going to Vila Cruzeiro

C Why do the TED speakers in **B** tell those stories? What points are they trying to make?

Brooklyn Bridge in New York City. New York is one of the most culturally diverse cities in the United States.

7E A sense of identity

COMMUNICATE A survey on identity

A What factors below do you think are important in giving you your sense of identity? Add your own idea and circle the level of importance.

Factors	Level of importance 1 = not important; 5 = very important
1 Where you were born	1 2 3 4 5
2 What language(s) you speak	1 2 3 4 5
3 Where you grew up	1 2 3 4 5
4 What culture(s) you are familiar with	1 2 3 4 5
5 Where you live now	1 2 3 4 5
6 Where your closest friends are from	1 2 3 4 5
7 Where your parents were born	1 2 3 4 5
8 What your job is	1 2 3 4 5
9 Where you spend most of your time	1 2 3 4 5
10 Your idea: _____	1 2 3 4 5

B Work in groups. Compare your ideas and create a list ranking the factors in **A**.

> **Making comparisons**
>
> … isn't as important as …
> … definitely has a stronger influence on …
> … probably has a bigger impact on …
> I think that … doesn't matter as much.

> For me, where I was born is …

> I don't think that … is so important to me.

C Tell the class about your group's top three factors and explain why you think they are the most important.

WRITING Writing a reflection

Look at the results above. Write one to two paragraphs on what you think about them and why you think they turned out this way.

> My group's results showed that where people spent most of their time was a very important factor in forming their sense of identity. I think that makes sense because it's where you become familiar with the people and culture …

Participants of the Cape Town Minstrels Carnival in South Africa

8 Transportation Solutions

"So we built something. I've got some of the pieces in my pocket here."

Sanjay Dastoor
Roboticist, TED speaker

UNIT GOALS

In this unit, you will ...

- talk about the future of transportation.
- read about some innovative commuting options.
- watch a TED Talk about an eco-friendly way of getting around town.

WARM UP

▶ **8.1** Watch part of Sanjay Dastoor's TED Talk. Answer the questions with a partner.

1 What kind of vehicle do you think the speaker is talking about?

2 Look through the unit. What types of transportation do you see?

Rush hour in the town of Antigua in Guatemala

8A Daily commutes

VOCABULARY Describing modes of transportation

A Check (✓) the words that are normally used with the types of transportation.

	ride	get on	get in	get off	take	drive
a bus	✓	✓		✓	✓	✓
a train						
a car						
a motorbike or bicycle						
the subway						
a plane						
a taxi						

B Complete the sentences using the words in the chart above.

1 I _____ my bicycle to work every day.

2 I sometimes _____ the bus two stops early and walk the rest of the way home.

3 The train was so packed this morning that I couldn't _____. I had to wait for the next one.

4 When I'm in a hurry, I usually _____ a taxi to work.

C Work with a partner. Which of the modes of transportation in **A** do you use? How often do you use them and where do you go?

> My dad drives me to school sometimes.

> I usually take the subway to go from my home to college.

LISTENING An unusual commute

> **Listening for frequency**
> We talk about our routines by using words expressing frequency.
>
> *Every morning, I …*   *I run … times a week.*   *After I get up, I usually …*

A ▶ **8.2** Cyril Burguiere has an unusual commute. Watch and discuss with a partner why he chose this type of commute.

B ▶ **8.2** Watch again. What does Burguiere enjoy most about his commute?

- ☐ being able to work out every morning
- ☐ saving time on commuting
- ☐ being close to nature
- ☐ meeting new people on his journey

C **CRITICAL THINKING**

Reflecting Work with a partner. How would you like to travel to school or work? Why?

Cyril Burguiere paddling down the Willamette River in Portland, Oregon

SPEAKING Talking about your daily routine

A ▶ **8.3** How do the speakers get to work?

A: Hey, you just moved to a new apartment, right? How do you get to work now?

B: It's quite complicated. I have to walk, take a bus to the train station, then take a train. Before this, I just walked a few minutes and then took a bus.

A: Wow! How long does it take for you to get to the office?

B: It takes over an hour. More sometimes. You have a short commute, don't you?

A: I drive, so it takes me about 20 minutes door to door, unless I'm stuck in traffic.

B: Have you ever thought about cycling to work?

A: That sounds pretty fun, but it would take an hour at least.

B: But it would be a great workout!

B Practice the conversation with a partner.

C Work with a partner. Describe your travel routines. What do you like or dislike about your commute? Use the expressions in blue above to help you.

> Most of the time, I go to school by bus because it's really convenient.

> I like walking to school. I get to …

8B The future of transportation

LANGUAGE FOCUS Making travel predictions

A ▶ **8.4** Read the information. What kinds of transportation do you think we will have in the future? How do you think current modes of transportation will change?

TRANSPORTATION IN THE FUTURE
Here are some ways we may be able to get around in the future.

AIR TRAVEL
By 2050, we might be able to travel between London and Sydney in under three hours, using planes that travel outside Earth's atmosphere.

EXPLORING SPACE
By 2030, ultra-luxury travelers might be able to travel into space for vacations.

DRIVERLESS CARS
By 2020, fully autonomous cars will be on the roads in some countries, allowing everyone to be a passenger.

HYPERLOOP
By 2020, people might be traveling between Los Angeles and Las Vegas in a high-speed pod powered by air pressure. The journey will take only about 30 minutes—less time than traveling by plane.

SKYTRAN
With more traffic congestion on the roads, more transportation will take to the air. SkyTran is one solution, where people travel in pods along rails in the air.

GIANT AIRSHIPS
By 2100, there might be giant airships carrying goods and taking passengers on cruises around the world.

B ▶ **8.5** Listen to the conversation. What are some pros and cons of space travel that the speakers mention? Discuss with a partner.

C ▶ **8.6** Watch and study the language in the chart.

Making predictions

Global car ownership **will** rise to 2.5 billion by 2050.
If the Hyperloop is built, it **will** definitely transform how we travel.
Tickets for space travel certainly **won't** be cheap.

Driverless cars **might** help make driving safer.
People **might** be able to take vacations in space by 2030.
Electric vehicles **might not** be as fast as fuel-powered cars, but they are better for the environment.

For more information on **will** and **might**, see Grammar Summary 8 on page 188.

D ▶ **8.5** Listen to the conversation in **B** again. Complete the sentences from the conversation.

1. "I read that by 2030, people _____ probably _____ their vacations in space."
2. "But they _____ test flights for the next few years."
3. "One day, we all _____ into space on day trips!"

E ▶ **8.7** Complete the information. Circle the correct words. Then listen and check your answers.

Companies and college students are testing ways to move people between cities by shooting them through giant tubes. This sounds like a concept from a sci-fi movie, but if the Hyperloop is built, people ¹(**are traveling** / **will be able to travel**) from Los Angeles to San Francisco (about 600 kilometers) in half an hour. There's also a possibility that it ²(**might be cheaper** / **is cheaper**) than rail travel.

A group of students at the Massachusetts Institute of Technology (MIT) is attempting to build the Hyperloop. John Mayo, project manager of the MIT Hyperloop Team, ³(**believes** / **might believe**) that some kind of Hyperloop—whether for transporting goods or passengers—will be a reality someday. He thinks engineers can figure out how to make it work. The real challenge, he says, ⁴(**was** / **will be**) whether it can be built cheaply enough and get government approval.

Visitors at a Hyperloop test site in Las Vegas

F Complete the sentences using the correct form of the words in parentheses with *will* or *might*.

1. There _____ certainly _____ (be) more electric vehicles on the roads in the next ten years.
2. As people buy more cars, there _____ (be) more congestion on the roads.
3. It's not certain, but the development of high-speed rail _____ (encourage) passengers to take the train instead of flying or driving.

SPEAKING Changes in global travel

Work in groups. Imagine what global travel will look like in the future. Write your predictions in the chart. Describe your predictions to the class.

In …	Predictions
5 years	
20 years	
50 years	
100 years	

> In 20 years, I think we'll have cars that can fly. These flying cars will be driverless.

> Within the next 50 years, people might be able to take day trips to space.

8C Unique commutes

PRE-READING Scanning

Scan the article. Name an example of each type of commute.

Land: _____ Water: _____ Air: _____

▶ 8.8

How do you get to school or work? For millions of people sitting in a traffic jam or standing on a crowded train, the daily commute probably isn't the best part of their day. But cars and trains aren't the only travel options. Here are some fun **alternative** modes of transportation you could consider.

ELECTRIC VEHICLES

For those who have a relatively short commute, you could consider getting an electric bike or scooter. An electric scooter has the advantage of being highly **portable**: small, and weighing around 20 kilograms—light enough to carry to the office and store under your desk. You'll just need to check if they are legal[1] in your area.

If you want a device straight out of a sci-fi movie, then you might consider a single-wheel electric scooter. One option is the RYNO, which is designed to be safe for use among **pedestrians**. At about 72 kilograms, the RYNO is less than half the weight of an average motorcycle. Its maximum speed is about the speed of a bicycle. And like other electric bikes and scooters, it can be **charged** anywhere.

WALKCAR

Can you imagine carrying your own transportation in your bag? If you want transportation for short distances—perhaps to get from home to the train station—the ultraportable WalkCar might be perfect for you. The WalkCar looks like a laptop and only weighs three kilograms—small and light enough to carry in a normal laptop bag. It's also incredibly easy to use—stand on it and it will start to move; move your weight to one side and it will change direction. The WalkCar will take you at a speed of up to 10 kilometers per hour and can travel 12 kilometers on one charge.

JETPACKS

If money is not an issue, how about a James Bond-style commute by personal jetpack? Weighing around 200 kilograms, jetpacks aren't exactly portable, but they're **guaranteed** to be a lot of fun and attract a lot of attention. Running on fuel, the jet engines allow the user to lift off the ground and fly in the air.

Personal water jetpacks are ideal for commutes on water of up to 50 kilometers. A hose[2] on your jetpack takes in water and releases it at high pressure to lift you up. You'll be able to fly up to 9 meters high, walk on water, or even dive as you travel to work.

Finally, for those who prefer staying dry on your commute, you can also fly on a traditional jetpack. One of the world's first practical jetpacks is the Martin Jetpack. Like the water jetpack, it's powered by fuel. Once you've strapped this tiny personal jet plane onto your back, you'll be able to travel up to 50 kilometers at a height of 1,000 meters. With a price tag of about $150,000, this is probably the most expensive option, but it will almost certainly be the coolest!

[1] **legal:** *adj.* allowed by law
[2] **hose:** *n.* a long tube that allows water or gas to flow through

Dean O'Malley, President of Jetpack America, flying on a water jetpack in Newport Beach, California

UNDERSTANDING MAIN IDEAS

What is the main purpose of the passage? Choose the most suitable option.

   a   to describe how some people are reducing their commuting times

   b   to persuade commuters to change the way they travel to work or school

   c   to suggest some creative and fun ways of commuting

UNDERSTANDING DETAILS

Complete the Venn diagram using the information below.

   a   can fit in a laptop bag
   b   users are able to fly
   c   rechargeable
   d   suitable for personal commutes
   e   weight: 20 kg and above
   f   fuel is needed to power the machine

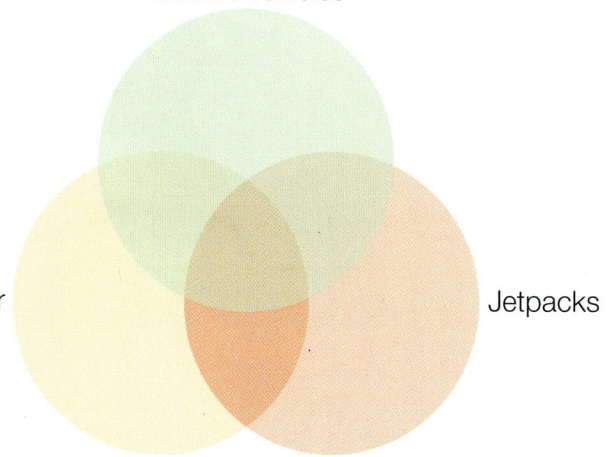

BUILDING VOCABULARY

A Complete the sentences using the correct form of the words in blue from the passage.

   1   It's important to make personal transportation devices _____ so people can take them everywhere they go.

   2   Electric cars that can be easily _____ are better for the environment.

   3   We need to create _____ methods of transportation that are more environmentally friendly.

   4   Driverless cars need to be tested to _____ the safety of passengers, _____, and other road users.

B   CRITICAL THINKING

   Evaluating Work with a partner. Discuss these questions.

   1   Which mode of transportation described in the passage would you recommend to people in your city? Why?

   2   What do you think are the pros and cons of each type of transportation mentioned in the passage?

   > I'd definitely recommend the WalkCar. It seems really easy to carry around.

   > A lot of people in my city drive. I think an electric bike would be a more eco-friendly option.

8D A skateboard, with a boost

TEDTALKS

SANJAY DASTOOR is the co-founder of Boosted Boards, a start-up that builds ultralight electric vehicles. Its aim is to create a highly portable and fun personal transportation device that anyone can use.

Sanjay Dastoor's idea worth spreading is that with a bit of creativity, you can turn an everyday object into a quick and eco-friendly way to get around the city.

PREVIEWING

Read the paragraph below. Circle the correct meaning for each **bold** word (1–4). You will hear these words in the TED Talk.

The **concept** behind this lightweight electric car is to create a new form of **sustainable** transportation that is good for the environment. It runs entirely on electricity, and its small size makes it highly **maneuverable**. The car's batteries give great **performance**, taking it up to 160 kilometers on a single charge.

1 A concept is (**an idea** / **a type of machine**).
2 Sustainable forms of energy (**use up** / **don't use up**) natural resources.
3 Something that is maneuverable is (**easy** / **difficult**) to move or direct.
4 The performance of an engine is (**how heavy it is** / **how well it functions**).

The Wheego electric car

109

VIEWING

A ▶ **8.9** Watch Part 1 of the TED Talk. Complete the information about Dastoor's electric vehicle.

	Electric skateboard
Charge time (minutes)	
Cost per 1,000 km ($)	
Top speed (km/h)	
Range (km)	

B ▶ **8.9** Watch Part 1 of the TED Talk again. Circle the correct words.

1 Dastoor and his team got some of the components from a (**toy store** / **car repair workshop**).

2 Parts of the skateboard were built with materials from (**electric bicycles** / **remote control airplanes**).

3 The skateboard is (**suitable** / **unsuitable**) for San Francisco's hilly terrain.

C ▶ **8.10** Watch Part 2 of the TED Talk. Check (✓) the benefits of the skateboard Dastoor mentions.

The skateboard _____.

☐ is simple to control   ☐ uses much less energy than a car

☐ is portable   ☐ charges quickly

☐ uses solar-powered batteries   ☐ is cheap to build

D CRITICAL THINKING

Evaluating Work with a partner. What disadvantages might there be in using an electric skateboard? Do you think the skateboard is suitable for your city? Why or why not?

VOCABULARY IN CONTEXT

A ▶ **8.11** Watch the excerpts from the TED Talk. Choose the correct meaning of the words.

B Complete the sentences with the words from the box.

novel	interact	leaving them with	carbon footprint

1 We can reduce our _____ by walking or taking public transportation.

2 Every year, we see _____ ideas about what transportation in the future may look like.

3 Have your audience think about your presentation by _____ a quote or question.

4 As machines become more intelligent, we will be able to _____ with them in different ways.

C Work with a partner. Have you seen any novel ideas of transportation that you would like to use? Where did you see them?

> I've seen people riding on electric unicycles. There's no seat or handle, but the unicycle is able to balance itself. I'd like to try it!

PRESENTATION SKILLS Signposting

Signposting means giving your audience directions about what you are going to say. You can do this at different stages of your presentation. Examples of signposting language include:

Starting
Today, I'd like to talk about …
Today, we're going to look at …

Moving on
So now I'm going to show you …
So now let's look at / move on to …

Concluding
So I'll leave you with / I'd like to finish by …
So, in summary / to summarize …
I want to summarize with …

A ▶ 8.12 Watch part of Sanjay Dastoor's TED Talk. Complete the signposting expressions that he uses. Then match them to their purpose.

1 "Today, _____ an electric vehicle …"   ○   ○ moving on
2 "_____ built something. I've got some of the pieces …" ○ ○ concluding
3 "So I'll _____ one of the most compelling facts …" ○   ○ starting

B ▶ 8.13 Watch the excerpts from two other TED Talks. Complete the signposting expressions that the speakers use. What do the speakers use them for?

1 "So now _____ perform a demonstration of this sock."
2 "And because the engineers I've worked with have taught me to become really in touch with my inner nerd, I _____ with an equation."

Dastoor believes that electric skateboards like this make commutes fun and efficient.

8E A new way to travel

COMMUNICATE Inventing a transportation device

A Work in groups. Brainstorm ideas for a new type of personal transportation. Think about who your invention will help the most, what people will be able to do with it, and how they will benefit.

B In your group, prepare a short description of your invention. Below are some words/phrases to help you.

easy to use	eco-friendly	comfortable
lightweight	remote-controlled	cheap to run
quick to charge	solar-powered	uses smart technology

C Present your group's invention to the class and persuade them to invest in your idea. Use signposting phrases to organize your presentation.

> **Persuasive language**
> With our creation, people no longer have to …   We strongly believe that this can help …
> … makes it much simpler for you to …   Our invention is better than … because …

> Our device is a type of bicycle that's designed for people who …

> The main advantage of our vehicle is …

WRITING Describing an invention

Create a poster describing your invention. Explain how it works and its benefits.

> Our invention is mainly for people who have difficulty climbing the stairs. All they have to do is attach this device to the handrail and …

A rider pedaling the Shweeb, a human-powered monorail, in New Zealand

9 New Words

" … so when does a word like *defriend* become real? "

Anne Curzan
Language historian, TED speaker

UNIT GOALS

In this unit, you will …

- talk about language change and attitudes toward it.
- read about new English words and why language changes.
- watch a TED Talk about what makes a word real.

WARM UP

▶ 9.1 Watch part of Anne Curzan's TED Talk. Answer the questions with a partner.

1. Do you know what *defriend* means?
2. Do you know any words that have become popular through social media? How did they become popular?

Students hold up cards to form an emoji during a football match in Columbus, Ohio.

9A Renewing language

VOCABULARY Describing language

A Read the paragraph below. Match the words in **bold** to their definitions.

Language is constantly changing. The meaning and the **usage** of some words can change. When more and more people use a word in a certain way, it may become **accepted** as **standard** language. One way we can observe language change is to look at how **slang** words become popular. Some people worry that these changes may **degrade** the language, but other people argue that language change is a natural process.

1 usage — make worse
2 accepted — informal language
3 standard — allowed or approved
4 slang — something that is widely regarded as a model
5 degrade — the way something is done or treated

B Work with a partner. Discuss these questions.

1 What groups of people do you use slang with? Do you use different kinds of slang when speaking with different groups of people?
2 Why do you think the usage of some words can change over time?

> I often use slang when talking to my friends and family.

> There are some slang expressions that I only use with my closest friends.

LISTENING Collecting words

> **Identifying the speaker's attitude**
> Adverbs at the beginning of sentences, such as *fortunately*, *honestly*, or *clearly*, show the speaker's attitude toward the idea that is being expressed.

A ▶ **9.2** Watch English professor Charles Browne talk about his work. Complete the information.

Professor Charles Browne feels that many English learners often don't know enough words to express themselves. A college-educated native speaker usually knows about ¹_____ words, but an average non-native learner in Japan, for example, only knows about ²_____ words. To help students overcome this problem, he has created the New General Service List (NGSL). By learning this list that includes ³_____ words, English learners will be able to understand ⁴_____ percent of everyday English.

B ▶ **9.3** Watch the rest of the interview. How might learning slang help English learners? Check (✓) the things Browne mentions.

☐ It gives students more opportunities to learn the language.

☐ It helps students keep up to date with the language.

☐ Students learn how to interact with people in informal situations.

C CRITICAL THINKING

Evaluating Work with a partner. How do you learn new words in English? Do you think the NGSL would be useful for you?

Professor Browne's NGSL has been translated into more than ten languages.

SPEAKING Talking about new words

A ▶ **9.4** What do the speakers think about newly created words?

A: When's our food coming? It's been almost half an hour!

B: I'm sure it will be here soon.

A: I hope so. I'm getting hangry!

B: Huh? Hangry? What does that mean?

A: It means I'm hungry and angry.

B: Then why don't you just say that? That would have been clear enough.

A: Well, it's quick and it gets to the point. New words like *hangry* can be really useful sometimes.

B: But what's the point of using a word most people don't understand?

A: Actually, I think more and more people are starting to use it. Maybe it'll be common one day!

B Practice the conversation with a partner.

C Work with a partner. Create a new word and tell your partner about it. Use the expressions in blue above to help you.

> My new word is "chairdrobe." I combined the words "chair" and "wardrobe."

> What does it mean?

9B Word evolution

LANGUAGE FOCUS Describing word trends

A ▶ 9.5 Read the information. Is there anything that surprised you? Why?

CHANGING WORDS

English, like all languages, is always changing. New words are being created, and meanings of existing words can change.

5 words whose meanings have changed

Word	Current meaning	Old meaning(s)
Cute	Pretty or charming	Intelligent or sharp
Fantastic	Wonderful	Unreal
Nice	Pleasant	Silly or simple. Then it came to mean lazy and after that, shy.
Pretty	Good-looking	Cunning. Later, it used to mean clever or skillful.
Naughty	Behaving badly, often used for children	To have nothing. Naughty people were people who were very poor.

Word of the year

 the "face with tears of joy" emoji
2015

vape (to use) an electronic cigarette
2014

selfie a photo you've taken of yourself, usually with a smartphone
2013

(Source: Oxford Dictionaries)

B ▶ 9.6 Listen to the conversation. How does the use of emojis help the speakers communicate better? Discuss with a partner.

C ▶ 9.7 Watch and study the language in the chart.

Talking about changes

Before email, people **used to** write and mail letters more frequently.
The word *awful* **used to** mean "full of fear or wonder," but now it means "very bad."

The word *silly* **didn't use to** have a negative meaning.
Cell phones **didn't use to** have big screens.

Did you use to look words up in a printed dictionary?
How **did you use to** keep in touch with your friends?

For more information on **used to**, see Grammar Summary 9 on page 188.

D ▶ **9.6** Listen to the conversation in **B** again. Complete the sentences with *used to* or *didn't use to*.

1 The woman _____ include emojis in her texts.
2 The man _____ send serious replies to his friend without realizing that his friend was joking.
3 The woman says that emojis _____ be common.
4 Facebook's "Like" button _____ include emojis.

E ▶ **9.8** Complete the information. Circle the correct words. Then listen and check your answers.

Before the fifth century, people living in Britain ¹(**don't speak** / **didn't use to speak**) English. They ²(**spoke** / **were speaking**) a Celtic language. Then, 1,500 years ago, people from what is now modern Germany and Denmark invaded. The languages these people spoke developed into Old English. In the 11th century, England was invaded again—this time by people from an area that's now part of France. For the next few hundred years, rich and important people ³(**speak** / **spoke**) French, while the poor ⁴(**communicate** / **communicated**) in Old English. The language continued to change: Thousands of French words were added, pronunciations that ⁵(**existed** / **didn't use to exist**) became common, and about 400 years ago, modern English was born.

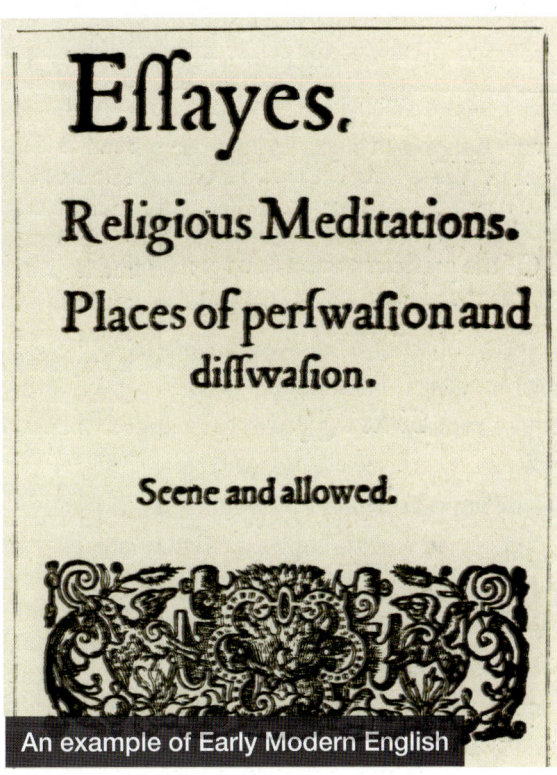
An example of Early Modern English

F Work with a partner. Discuss these questions.

1 Do you know any words or phrases in your own language that used to be popular but aren't anymore? Why did people stop using them?
2 What are some examples of words and phrases that you use now but didn't use to say?

SPEAKING Talking about changes in meaning

Work with a partner. You are going to read and talk about words that had a different meaning in the past. **Student A:** Turn to page 167. **Student B:** Turn to page 169.

What did *bully* use to mean?

Well, in the 16th century, the word meant ...

9C Language change

PRE-READING Skimming

Skim the article. What is one difference between slang and a standard form of language?

▶ 9.9

1   In 2013, Harris Academy—a school in south London—**banned** its students from using slang. Posters around the school showed a list of slang words that students weren't allowed to use, such as
5   *ain't* and *like*. The move led to a debate on whether it is necessary to control the way students speak.

    The creation of slang is one way languages change. Slang, or informal language, usually changes more **rapidly** than standard language.
10 For example, the word *groovy*, meaning "great," used to be very popular in the 1960s and '70s. But by 1980, people had stopped using it. Throughout history, changes in language have received much criticism. In 1789, Benjamin Franklin, one of the
15 founding fathers of the United States, wrote about his objections to words such as *notice* and *progress* being used as verbs.

WHY DO WE USE SLANG?

One important reason we use slang is to show
20 others that we belong to a group. When only a particular group of people use and understand certain words and phrases, it **strengthens** their sense of identity within that group. Each different group—teenagers, the media, and so on—has its
25 own set of slang. Another reason for using slang is to communicate an idea in a more colorful or humorous[1] way. For example, the phrase *jump ship* creates a stronger image than the more standard *leave an organization*. In addition, slang often allows
30 us to express complex ideas effectively. The word *frenemy* (someone who pretends to be a friend, but is really an enemy) **conveys** its meaning more quickly than standard language.

In the age of social media and the Internet, slang
35 terms are created faster than ever. Often, Internet slang words are created to make messages faster and easier to type. Some examples include *btw* (by the way) and *YOLO* (you only live once).

IS SLANG DEGRADING OUR LANGUAGE?

40 Some people feel strongly against the use of slang. Teachers at Harris Academy were worried that slang would prevent their students from learning how to read, write, and express themselves correctly. They

42,000 profile photos of social media users forming a giant hashtag. The hashtag is often used on social media to label posts, sometimes in a humorous way.

thought this might cause problems for students
45 when they eventually went on to apply to universities or to look for jobs. David Lammy, a British politician, supports the school's decision. He feels that people need to know when to use formal and informal language.
50 However, some people think differently. Linguist Tony Thorne sees slang as a way for speakers of a language to show their creativity and humor. He argues that slang is important in social interactions, enabling us to express who we are and the
55 communities we belong to. And—contrary to what some believe—slang is not a new phenomenon.²

As Thorne explains, "Slang has not become more prevalent,³ simply more public." In today's highly connected world, slang has become more
60 **noticeable** because of better tools to observe language change.

Perhaps the concerns raised by critics can be solved by making people aware of when to use certain forms of language. As long as people use
65 slang in the right situations, there may not be a need to completely discourage it.

[1] **humorous:** *adj.* funny, amusing
[2] **phenomenon:** *n.* an unusual event
[3] **prevalent:** *adj.* common

UNDERSTANDING MAIN IDEAS

Check (✓) the sentences that the author would probably agree with.

☐ Harris Academy's ban on slang words was surprising because slang didn't use to receive so much criticism.

☐ We use slang to show people we are part of a group.

☐ It's okay to use slang during a job interview because it shows your personality.

☐ People need to learn how to switch between formal and informal forms of language depending on the situation.

UNDERSTANDING DETAILS

Match the slang words to the points they are used to illustrate.

1 groovy ○   ○ Slang can express an idea in a more interesting way than standard language.
2 jump ship ○   ○ Texts and messages sent online are usually short and easy to type.
3 frenemy ○   ○ Slang words sometimes appear and disappear quickly.
4 btw ○   ○ Slang allows speakers to combine and express several different ideas at once.

UNDERSTANDING ARGUMENTS

Complete the arguments for and against slang.

Arguments for slang	Arguments against slang
1 strengthens our _____ within a group	1 prevents young people from learning how to _____ properly
2 allows people to express themselves in a(n) _____ way	2 makes it difficult for young people when they apply to _____ or look for _____
3 enables people to communicate _____ ideas effectively	

BUILDING VOCABULARY

A Complete the sentences using the correct form of the words in blue from the passage.

1 Emojis can _____ messages in a fun and interesting way.

2 If you _____ something, you stop people from doing it.

3 Listening to news in English can _____ your English language skills.

4 A language can die when the number of people speaking it decreases _____ or when it's no longer taught to younger people.

5 Some changes in language aren't _____ because they happen over hundreds of years.

B CRITICAL THINKING

Reflecting Work with a partner. What do you think about slang? Would you encourage people to use it? Why or why not?

9D What makes a word "real"?

TEDTALKS

ANNE CURZAN is an English professor at the University of Michigan. She is **fascinated** by how people use words. Although people are sometimes **bothered** by changes in language, she points out that everyone has the **authority** to decide how it changes. And these changes, she believes, help to keep a language **robust**.

Anne Curzan's idea worth spreading is that a word is real when it's understood by a community of people, and that dictionary editors must pay close attention to trends in language over time.

PREVIEWING

Read the paragraphs above. Match each **bold** word to its meaning. You will hear these words in the TED Talk.

1 strong _____

2 the power to decide or control _____

3 concerned or annoyed _____

4 very interested in something _____

VIEWING

A ▶ 9.10 Watch Part 1 of the TED Talk. Answer questions 1 to 3.

1 Why do you think Anne Curzan's dinner companion questioned whether *defriend* is a real word?

   a He had never heard the word before.

   b He didn't know the meaning of the word.

   c It's a new word that he doesn't like.

2 According to Anne Curzan, what do most people mean when they say a word isn't real?

   a It isn't in a standard dictionary.

   b It's only used in certain places.

   c Only a few people use it.

3 What does Anne Curzan suggest when she says that even the most critical people don't usually question dictionaries?

   a People have become less interested in using dictionaries.

   b People tend to think that dictionaries are always accurate or all the same.

   c People need to learn how to use dictionaries in the correct way.

B ▶ 9.11 Watch Part 2 of the TED Talk. Circle the correct words.

1 Dictionary editors (**study historical language records** / **watch how we use language**) in order to identify trends.

2 Curzan gives *LOL* as an example of a phrase that will probably (**remain popular** / **be used less frequently in the future**).

3 Dictionary editors are (**sure that** / **unsure if**) the phrase *YOLO* is a fad.

4 People who observe language usually (**predict** / **notice**) the same things, but have different attitudes toward them.

C ▶ 9.12 Watch Part 3 of the TED Talk. Check (✓) the sentences that Anne Curzan would probably agree with.

☐ There's no problem with using *impact* as a verb and *invite* as a noun.

☐ Language change helps to keep a language alive and strong.

☐ Dictionary editors need greater authority in order to create accurate language guides for people.

☐ If a slang word is used and understood by a group of people, it's a real word.

D **CRITICAL THINKING**

Evaluating Work with a partner. Can you think of any ways people could challenge Anne Curzan's view on language change?

> Slang can be harmful because only a select group of people understand it, so it leaves people out.

VOCABULARY IN CONTEXT

A ▶ 9.13 Watch the excerpts from the TED Talk. Choose the correct meaning of the words.

B Work with a partner. Discuss these questions.

1 How do you keep up your English language skills?

2 What expressions have you noticed coming into prominence in your language?

3 Are there any slang words that you think will make it into a standard dictionary in the future?

> I keep up my English language skills by watching movies in English.

PRESENTATION SKILLS Closing the loop

> One good way of organizing your presentation is to end by going back to the question(s) that you asked at the beginning. This is called closing the loop.

A ▶ **9.14** Watch the beginning of Anne Curzan's TED Talk. Check (✓) the questions that she asks.

☐ What makes a word real?

☐ How accurate are dictionaries?

☐ When do new words become real?

☐ Who makes decisions about words?

B ▶ **9.15** Watch the end of Curzan's TED Talk. How does she close the loop and answer the questions in **A**? Discuss with a partner.

C Choose one of these topics: expressions that used to be popular in your language, or expressions that you didn't use to say. What question could you ask your audience at the beginning? How would you answer your question and close the loop?

D Work with a partner. Practice closing the loop by giving a one-minute presentation on the topic you chose in **C**.

French linguist Alain Rey (far right) with the authors of Lexik des Cités, a dictionary of French suburban slang

9E What does it mean?

COMMUNICATE Guessing meanings

A You are going to play a guessing game about the meaning of some new English words. Look at the example below.

> **Example:** *binge watch*
> a to eat as you watch a TV program
> b to look at someone's food and feel jealous
> c to watch multiple episodes of a TV program continuously

> The phrase *binge watch* refers to watching multiple episodes of a TV program continuously. Here's how it can be used in a sentence: *This TV show is so exciting! I think I'm going to binge watch the entire season.*

B Work in groups. **Group A:** Turn to page 167. **Group B:** Turn to page 169. Read about three words/phrases and create two incorrect meanings for each one.

C Present your definitions for each word/phrase to the other group. Describe each definition by giving an example of how the word/phrase can be used, where it came from, who created it, and so on. The other group has to guess the correct meaning.

> **Describing word meanings**
> *This word/phrase comes from …*   *This word/phrase refers to …*
> *People use this word/phrase to …* *Here's an example sentence: …*

WRITING Making an argument

Do you think the Internet is degrading the English language? Write a few paragraphs on whether you agree or disagree, and give reasons for your view.

> I think that language change is something we should accept. Although some people may argue that Internet slang is causing us to lose the ability to speak and write properly, I feel that …

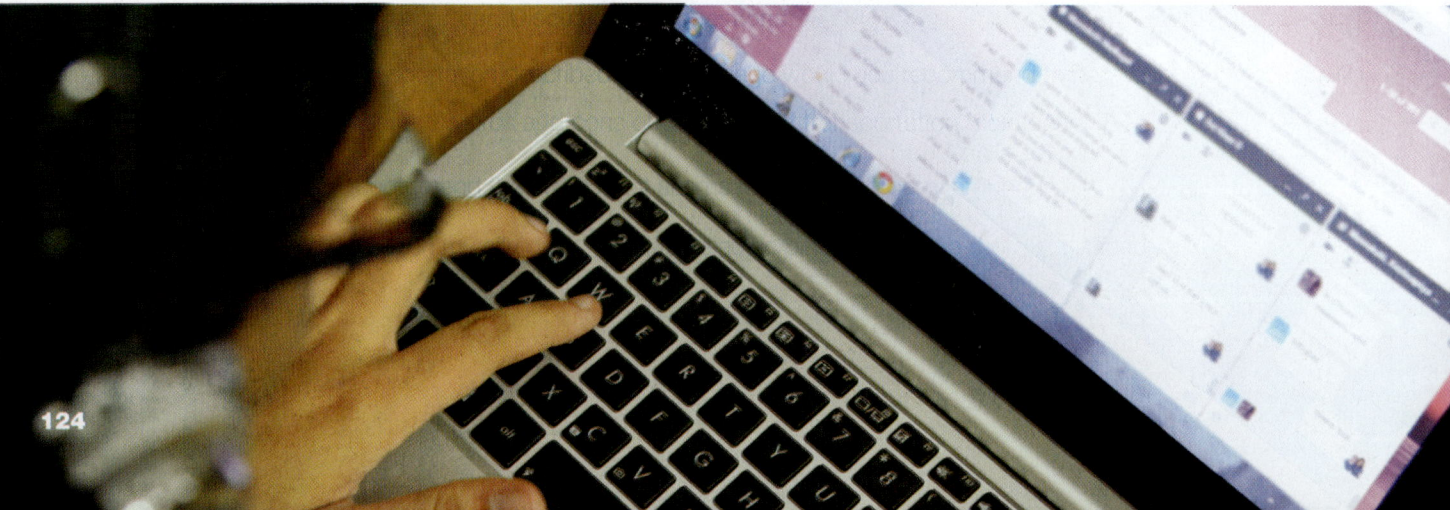

Presentation 3

MODEL PRESENTATION

A Complete the transcript of the presentation using the words in the box.

| used to | cultures | has been living | background |
| a lot in common | might not | didn't use to | definitely |

Hello, everybody. I'm Olivia. I'm glad to be here this afternoon. Do you have a friend with an interesting ¹_____? Today, I'd like to tell you about a friend of mine. I'll tell you a bit about her, where she's from, and why we're good friends.

You know, I ²_____ do much exercise. Then, a couple of years ago, I joined a fitness club. On my first day there, I met Raquel. After the gym, we had coffee together and quickly became good friends. I think that's because we have ³_____—we both like to keep fit and love trying different food—especially spicy food. And we love the ocean; in the summer, we like to hang out at the beach and go surfing at least once a month. Raquel was born in Mexico, but ⁴_____ here since she was ten. Her mother is Mexican and her dad is American, so she speaks both Spanish and English. That's something different about us: Even though I ⁵_____ study it, my Spanish is terrible! Another thing that's different is her background—Raquel's from two countries and has experience and knowledge of two ⁶_____. I think that's really cool.

So, now you know a bit about my friend Raquel. Although we ⁷_____ always live in the same city in the future, I think we'll ⁸_____ stay friends. Thanks for listening to me.

B ▶ **P.3** Watch the presentation and check your answers.

C ▶ **P.3** Review the list of presentation skills from Units 1–9 below. Which does the speaker use? Check (✓) them as you watch again. Then compare with a partner.

The speaker …
- helps the audience visualize by
  - doing a demonstration ☐
  - giving interesting facts ☐
  - using visuals ☐
- comments on visuals ☐
- opens with an interesting fact ☐
- asks the audience questions ☐
- ends with a hope for the future ☐
- engages with the audience ☐
- uses a story to personalize the message ☐
- uses signposting language ☐
- closes the loop ☐

D Do you remember the question Olivia asks at the beginning? What phrase does she use at the end to close the loop? Underline them in the script.

YOUR TURN

A You are going to plan and give a short presentation about someone you know a lot about or are close to. It could be a member of your family, a close friend, or someone famous. Make notes in the chart below.

> Who is it?
>
>
> Details (how you know the person, where they are from, languages they speak, etc.)

B Look at the useful phrases in the box below. Think about which ones you will need in your presentation.

> **Useful phrases**
>
> | | |
> |---|---|
> | Describing someone's background: | He's/She's from …
 He/She was born in …
 He/She has lived in … |
> | Describing similarities and differences: | We both like / love to …
 We are different in the way we … |
> | Describing relationships: | We have been friends since/for …
 I got to know him/her when … |

C Work with a partner. Take turns giving your presentation using your notes. Use some of the presentation skills from Units 1–9. As you listen, check (✓) each skill your partner uses.

> The speaker …
> - helps the audience visualize by
>   - doing a demonstration ☐
>   - giving interesting facts ☐
>   - using visuals ☐
> - comments on visuals ☐
> - opens with an interesting fact ☐
> - asks the audience questions ☐
> - ends with a hope for the future ☐
> - engages with the audience ☐
> - uses a story to personalize the message ☐
> - uses signposting language ☐
> - closes the loop ☐

D Give your partner some feedback on their talk. Include at least two things you liked and one thing that could be improved.

> That was great. You used signposting language and showed lots of visuals. But I think you need to engage the audience more.

10 Understanding Emotions

" I want to bring emotions back into our digital experiences. "

Rana el Kaliouby
Computer scientist, TED speaker

UNIT GOALS

In this unit, you will …

- talk about emotions and how they influence us.
- read about the applications of technology that can recognize our emotions.
- watch a TED Talk about how emotion-sensing technology can help us.

WARM UP

▶ **10.1** Watch part of Rana el Kaliouby's TED Talk. Answer the questions with a partner.

1 What do you think is happening? What is the machine able to do?

2 In what ways might this technology be useful?

Two boys fishing in a stream in Thailand

10A Our emotions

VOCABULARY Describing feelings

A Are the words below more positive or more negative? Write the letters in the diagram.

a shocked b delighted c lonely d overwhelmed
e frustrated f surprised g confused h relieved

Positive   Negative

B Complete the sentences using the words in **A**.

1 I was _____ that my brother, who works overseas, was coming home for the holidays.

2 I haven't been getting much sleep lately because I've been _____ with schoolwork.

3 I was _____ when I heard about the damage that the earthquake caused.

4 People who live in a different country from their family and friends may feel _____ at times.

C Work with a partner. Give an example of a time you experienced each of the emotions in **A**.

> Yesterday, I was frustrated because I couldn't figure out what was wrong with my computer.

> Last week, I was delighted when I received a gift from my friend in China.

LISTENING Dealing with emotions

> **Giving examples**
> Here are some phrases we can use when giving examples to elaborate on our points.
> *Some of the most common …*   *For instance, …*   *Take … for example.*

A ▶ **10.2** Watch guidance counselor Craig Albrightson talk about his work. What are some of the challenges he says his students usually encounter?

- ☐ uncertainty in deciding career paths
- ☐ family problems
- ☐ managing relationships with schoolmates
- ☐ adjusting to their new surroundings

B ▶ **10.3** Watch the rest of the interview. Why does Albrightson believe that it's important to manage our emotions well?

a It gives us self-confidence.
b It helps us make good decisions in life.
c It helps us be more sensitive to other people's feelings.

Craig Albrightson helps his students overcome their difficulties.

C CRITICAL THINKING

Inferring Work with a partner. What do you think a guidance counselor needs to be like? Why?

SPEAKING Talking about managing emotions

A ▶ **10.4** How do the speakers react to the situation?

A: Hey, look. That guy just cut in line. Unbelievable!
B: Oh, yeah, I see him. Oh, well.
A: Does he think we're all just standing here for fun? What nerve!
B: It happens sometimes. At least it isn't a really long line, so we won't have to wait too long.
A: I hate it when people do that. It really annoys me.
B: Yeah. But it's no big deal.
A: I'll go and tell him he can't do that.
B: Hey, calm down. It's not worth getting angry about. Just let it go.

B Practice the conversation with a partner.

C Work with a partner. What annoys you? When your friends or family members get annoyed, how do you deal with it? Use the expressions in blue above to help you.

> I get annoyed when people don't say thank you.

> The other day, someone on the bus stepped on my foot but didn't apologize.

10B Emotional intelligence

LANGUAGE FOCUS Discussing EQ and jobs

A ▶ 10.5 Read the information. Have you ever taken an EQ test?

What is emotional intelligence?

Emotional intelligence is the ability to understand how people feel and react to things. It is also being able to use this ability to solve problems and make good judgments.

People with high emotional intelligence are able to …
- control their urges to do something
- recognize their strengths and weaknesses
- build strong relationships with others
- understand the emotions of other people

A survey showed that people who often had to interact with clients or employees usually have higher average EQ scores.

- 44 military personnel
- 47 students
- 55 technicians
- 68 salespeople
- 71 managers and executives
- 74 customer support personnel

Scale of EQ scores: high 80 – 60 – 40 – 20 – 0 low

B ▶ 10.6 Listen to the conversation. Where did the speakers take their EQ tests?

C ▶ 10.7 Watch and study the language in the chart.

Reporting other people's speech and thoughts	
"We're going to do a study on EQ." →	They said they were going to do a study on EQ.
"We'd like you to take an EQ test." →	They asked me to take an EQ test.
"I have an interview next week." →	He told me he had an interview next week.
"I'll be in touch after the interview." →	She promised to be in touch after the interview.
"Remember to email me the document." →	He reminded me to email him the document.

Some companies believe that people with good emotional skills make better workers.
Psychologist Daniel Goleman thinks that emotional intelligence is as important as cognitive intelligence.
According to researchers, there is no significant difference between men's and women's level of EQ.

For more information on **reported speech**, see Grammar Summary 10 on pages 189–190.

D ▶ **10.6** Listen to the conversation in **B** again. Complete the sentences from the conversation.

1 "They just _____ get in touch."
2 "They _____ me that the EQ test really _____ them find people who are suited for the job."
3 "Well, I _____ good at dealing with people."

E Write the following sentences using reported speech. Use the correct form of the words in parentheses.

1 "Do you know the difference between EQ and IQ?"
   He _____asked if I knew the difference between EQ and IQ_____. (ask)
2 "People with low EQ usually show less empathy."
   He _____. (believe)
3 "We need people with good self-management skills."
   They _____. (say)
4 "Remember to write a cover letter before sending your job application."
   She _____. (remind)

F Work with a partner. Take turns asking the questions below. Then share your partner's responses with another pair.

1 What do you usually do in stressful situations?
2 Do you think you have a high EQ? Why or why not?

> Andy said that he usually talks to someone when he's feeling stressed.

> Sarah told me that …

Being stuck in traffic can be a stressful situation for some people.

SPEAKING Talking about EQ in jobs

A Work with a partner. Look at the list of jobs below. Color in the stars based on how important you think having a high EQ is for the job (1 star = least important).

☆☆☆☆☆ nurse   ☆☆☆☆☆ CEO
☆☆☆☆☆ actor/actress   ☆☆☆☆☆ waiter/waitress
☆☆☆☆☆ taxi driver   ☆☆☆☆☆ journalist
☆☆☆☆☆ accountant   ☆☆☆☆☆ salesperson
☆☆☆☆☆ politician   ☆☆☆☆☆ computer programmer

B Share your ratings with the class, and explain why you think it's important for people in some jobs to have a high EQ.

> We think it's very important for CEOs to have a high EQ because they need to …

> We think nurses need a high EQ because …

131

10C Emotion in technology

PRE-READING Skimming

Skim the passage. How are some technology companies using Dr. Ekman's work?

▶ 10.8

1   People have long imagined a world where we interact with computers and robots as if they were normal human beings. Science fiction movies such as *Her* and *Chappie* show computers and robots that think and feel just like humans. While scenarios like these exist only in the movies for now, we may be getting close to making technology emotionally intelligent.

2   The first step toward this is understanding what emotions are. It's a complicated area of study. Scientists are often unable to define emotions in exact terms, even though we generally understand what people mean when they say they're sad or happy.

3   Back in the 1950s, few scientists studied emotion. But American psychologist Paul Ekman saw a lot of potential in this field. He began analyzing facial expressions, and compiled a list of over 5,000 muscle movements. These muscle movements **combine** to form our different expressions. His discovery of micro[1] expressions—facial expressions that last only a fraction of a second—allows us to read the emotions that people try to hide. A number of technology companies have now started to use Dr. Ekman's work to create software that recognizes human facial expressions. By analyzing thousands of different faces, the software learns to recognize different emotions with greater and greater accuracy.

4   There are many possible uses of emotion-sensing technology. Dr. Chieko Asakawa, a researcher at Carnegie Mellon University, has been blind since the age of 14. She has been developing a smartphone app that might be able to help people with disabilities. Using the smartphone's camera and audio, the app helps the user navigate their environment. It also recognizes people's faces and facial expressions as they approach. Dr. Asakawa is working to refine the app to enable it to read people's moods.

5   Another use of emotion-sensing technology can be illustrated through human-shaped robots like Pepper. Launched in Japan in 2015,

Pepper the robot is able to adapt its behavior to people's personalities and preferences.

Pepper is an interactive **companion** robot. It's capable of recognizing basic human emotions and responding appropriately. For example, it **comforts** someone when it senses the person is sad, or cracks a joke when the person is feeling playful. In Japan, Pepper is already serving customers in retail stores.

6   Although the idea of emotionally intelligent devices may sound fascinating, this technology can create some major challenges. The issue of **privacy** is something that many people, including Paul Ekman, are concerned about. For example, as we walk on the streets, devices and scanners could record our facial expressions without our knowledge. This could allow many people to monitor or view our feelings without **permission**. It may leave us no control over who we share our feelings with. However, if we can negotiate[2] these challenges successfully, there could be many benefits for all of us if our devices become a little more human.

[1] **micro:** *adj.* tiny
[2] **negotiate:** *v.* get around something successfully

UNDERSTANDING MAIN IDEAS

Match the paragraphs in the passage to the most suitable headings.

1 Paragraph 3   ○   ○ Challenges and Concerns
2 Paragraphs 4–5   ○   ○ The Beginning of Emotion Research
3 Paragraph 6   ○   ○ Applications of Emotion-Sensing Technology

UNDERSTANDING DETAILS

Complete the concept map about emotionally intelligent technology.

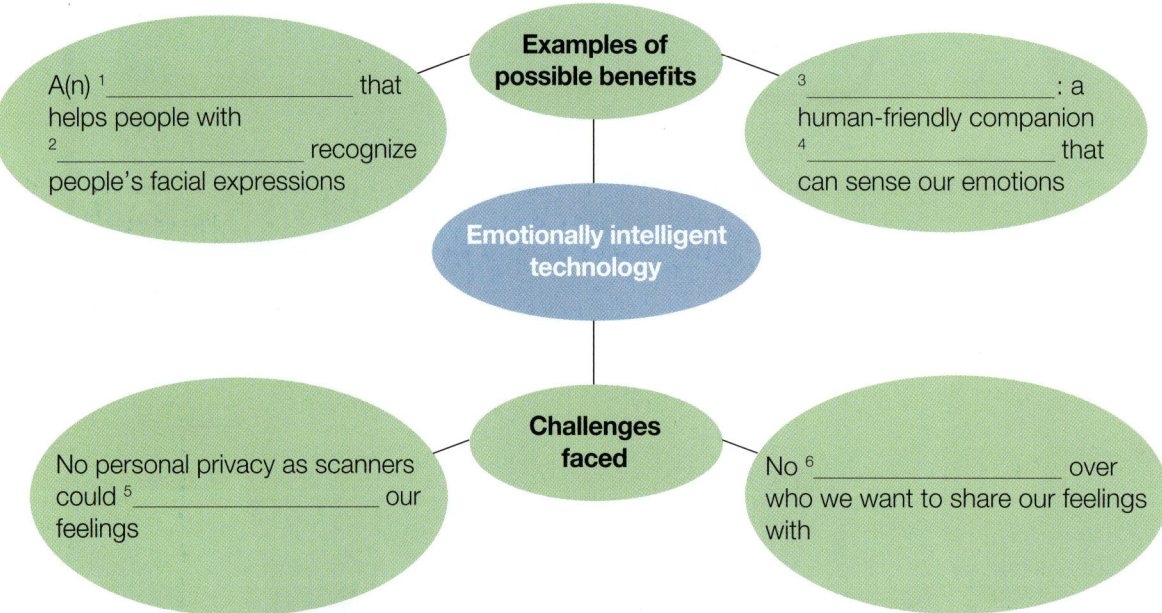

BUILDING VOCABULARY

A Complete the sentences. Circle the correct words.

1 It's usually necessary to get someone's (**privacy** / **permission**) before taking their photo.

2 The movements of our facial muscles can (**combine** / **comfort**) to express complex emotions, such as being sad and angry at the same time.

3 A robot that is able to work and live alongside humans could make a good (**companion** / **privacy**) for people who live alone.

4 When you (**combine** / **comfort**) someone, you make them feel less sad or worried.

B CRITICAL THINKING

Applying Work with a partner. Besides the groups of people mentioned in the passage, who else do you think might benefit from the use of emotion-sensing technology? How could the technology help them?

> I think people who want to improve their EQ could use this technology to …

> I believe this technology could help people who have difficulty with …

10D This app knows how you feel

TEDTALKS

RANA EL KALIOUBY is a computer scientist and co-founder of a tech start-up. Her **mission** is to **humanize** technology; she's developing technology that is able to recognize even **subtle** facial expressions. She believes this kind of technology has the **potential** to benefit us in many ways.

Rana el Kaliouby's idea worth spreading is that by teaching computers how to register emotions, we can eventually bring more feelings into the digital experience and form personal connections with our devices.

PREVIEWING

Read the paragraphs above. Circle the correct meaning for each **bold** word (1–4). You will hear these words in the TED Talk.

1 If you are on a mission, you are working (**on a team** / **toward a certain goal**).
2 To humanize something is to (**make it user-friendly** / **give it the characteristics of a person**).
3 Something that is subtle (**is** / **isn't**) easily recognized.
4 If a person has a lot of potential, the person has (**the ability to do well** / **a lot of power**).

VIEWING

A ▶ **10.9** Watch Part 1 of the TED Talk. Complete the timeline showing Rana el Kaliouby's experience. Note the events (a–d) on the diagram.

a She formed a team to create technologies that can read and respond to our emotions.
b She thought about how emotionally intelligent technologies could be useful for people.
c She left Egypt to do a Ph.D. in computer science.
d She found it frustrating that she couldn't communicate her emotions accurately online to her family.

B ▶ **10.10** Watch Part 2 of the TED Talk. Complete the labels.

The box identifies the person's ¹_____.

The points track the main features of her face: eyebrows, ²_____, ³_____, and nose.

The device can recognize other emotions like surprise and ⁵_____.

The green bar ⁴_____ as she smiles, indicating happiness.

C ▶ **10.11** Read the sentences below and predict the team's findings. Then watch Part 3 of the TED Talk and check your answers.

1 In the United States, women are 40 percent (**more / less**) expressive than men.

2 In the United Kingdom, women are (**less expressive than / as expressive as**) men.

3 Women in their 20s (**frown / smile**) a lot more than men the same age.

4 People are (**more expressive in the morning / expressive all the time**).

D ▶ **10.12** Watch Part 4 of the TED Talk. Match each tech idea to its general purpose.

1 glasses that read emotions   ○   ○ safety

2 apps that track your learning pace ○   ○ education

3 cars that detect if you're tired   ○   ○ health

4 fridges that auto-lock   ○   ○ helping people with disabilities

E CRITICAL THINKING

Evaluating Work with a partner. Which statement best summarizes Rana el Kaliouby's conclusion?

1 We should accept that we will use technology and devices more in the future. Instead of reducing the amount of time we spend on them, we should try to build emotions into technology.

2 Besides limiting how much we use digital devices, we should also make them more human.

VOCABULARY IN CONTEXT

A ▶ **10.13** Watch the excerpts from the TED Talk. Choose the correct meaning of the words.

B Work with a partner. How many years down the line do you think emotion-sensing technology will become a part of our reality? What are the advantages and disadvantages?

> We rely on technology a lot these days, so I think …

> A few years down the line, emotion-sensing technology will definitely …

PRESENTATION SKILLS Giving a demonstration

> Use clear language when you give a demonstration to your audience. Here are some phrases to use.
>
> So, we're going to … / So, today, I'm going to … / So, first of all, …
>
> (And) Then … / Now … / Next, …
>
> As you can see, … / Can you see …?
>
> Finally, …

A ▶ **10.14** Watch part of Rana el Kaliouby's TED Talk. Complete the sentences with the phrases she uses to give a demonstration.

1 "_____, the algorithm has essentially found Cloe's face …"

2 "So _____ test the machine."

3 "So _____, give me your poker face."

4 "So _____ the green bar go up as she smiles."

B ▶ **10.14** Watch again. What is the purpose of each sentence in **A**? Write the letters. Letters may be used more than once.

a giving an introduction	b sequencing events	c clarifying what's happening

1 _____   2 _____   3 _____   4 _____

Rana el Kaliouby's app is able to detect subtle expressions.

10E Emotion-sensing devices

COMMUNICATE Applications of emotion-sensing technology

A Work in groups. Come up with an idea for an emotion-sensing device. Some ideas for devices are given in the box.

> fridge   car   smartphone   desk   lamp   glasses   TV

B Think about what the device will do. Why is there a need for it? How will it help people?

> A lamp that dims the light when it senses that we're tired can help us relax and get ready for bed at night.

C Share your idea with three other groups. Get them to rate your creation and give reasons for their answers. Note their responses in the chart.

Ratings: 1 – Yes, it would be great!   2 – Yes, it may be a good idea.   3 – No, probably not.   4 – No, absolutely not!

Group	Rating	Reason

D Take turns reporting the results of your survey to the class. What did people like best about your idea? How could you improve on it?

> **Reporting language**
>
> Based on the results, ...   What we've found is ...
> The majority of people feel that ...   Looking at the survey results, ...

WRITING Expressing an opinion

Do you think there is a need for technology to be able to recognize emotions? Use one example of a tech device in this unit to support your view. Explain how it could be beneficial, or highlight any concerns.

> I think technology that is able to recognize human emotions could be useful. For example, a car that can sense when we are tired might be able to improve road safety.

A driver-fatigue warning sign in Australia

11 Leaders and Thinkers

> " I learned early on that if you can run one company, you can run any company. "

Richard Branson
Entrepreneur, TED speaker

UNIT GOALS

In this unit, you will …

- talk about business and leadership.
- read about lessons in business management.
- watch a TED Talk about Richard Branson's ideas on succeeding in business.

WARM UP

▶ **11.1** Watch part of Richard Branson's TED Talk. Answer the questions with a partner.

1 Have you heard of the Virgin Group? Do you know any Virgin companies?

2 What business leaders would you like to meet? Why?

139

Howard Schultz, CEO of Starbucks, with employees in Mexico

11A Business leaders

VOCABULARY Doing business

A ▶ 11.2 Complete the sentences using the words in the box. Then listen and check your answers.

| reputation | careers | manage staff | run a company | ruthless |

1 Some people believe that to get to the top, you may have to be _____.
2 Many entrepreneurs gave up successful _____ to start their own businesses.
3 If you can _____ well and take care of their needs, your company is more likely to grow.
4 It's very important for companies to protect the _____ of their businesses.
5 It takes a lot of hard work to _____ successfully and grow it into a global business.

B Match the words to form phrases.

1 start   ○   ○ a competitor
2 take   ○   ○ a business
3 work out   ○   ○ a risk
4 go against   ○   ○ a business strategy

C Work with a partner. Would you like to run a company? How comfortable are you with taking risks?

> I'd like to run a small website design business.

> I don't think I'm interested in running a company.

LISTENING Starting a business

> **Listening for sequence of events**
> Time expressions help us understand the order of events.
> **After** I graduated, …   **Since** 2005, …   **Then** I went to …

A ▶ **11.3** Watch entrepreneur Priscilla Shunmugam talk about her journey to start her own business. Order the events from 1 to 5.

_____ She traveled to London.

_____ She practiced law for a few years.

_____ She started Ong Shunmugam.

_____ She was dissatisfied with her career.

_____ She learned how to sew and took courses in fashion design.

B ▶ **11.4** Watch the rest of the interview. What personal goals does Shunmugam mention?

☐ to preserve traditional Asian history through her designs

☐ to explore Western designs in her dresses

☐ to be a mentor to aspiring designers

☐ to start a design school

A model wearing one of Priscilla Shunmugam's designs.

C **CRITICAL THINKING**

Predicting Work with a partner. What kinds of challenges do you think Priscilla Shunmugam faced when she set up her business?

SPEAKING Talking about what makes a good leader

A ▶ **11.5** Which speaker do you agree with more?

A: What do you think makes a good leader?

B: I think my manager at my previous job was a good leader. He was always confident in his decisions.

A: Yeah, I guess that's pretty important.

B: And I think you have to care about the people who work for you.

A: Really? But there are lots of ruthless leaders out there.

B: Maybe, but people won't like working with them. Great leaders need to be able to inspire people. I think that's the most important thing.

B Practice the conversation with a partner.

C Work with a partner. What qualities do you think are most important for a leader? Why? Use the expressions in blue above to help you.

> I think one quality every leader should have is passion.

> Definitely. In my opinion, a good leader also needs to be humble.

11B Being a leader

LANGUAGE FOCUS What makes a CEO?

A ▶ **11.6** Read the survey results. What other questions would you ask the CEOs?

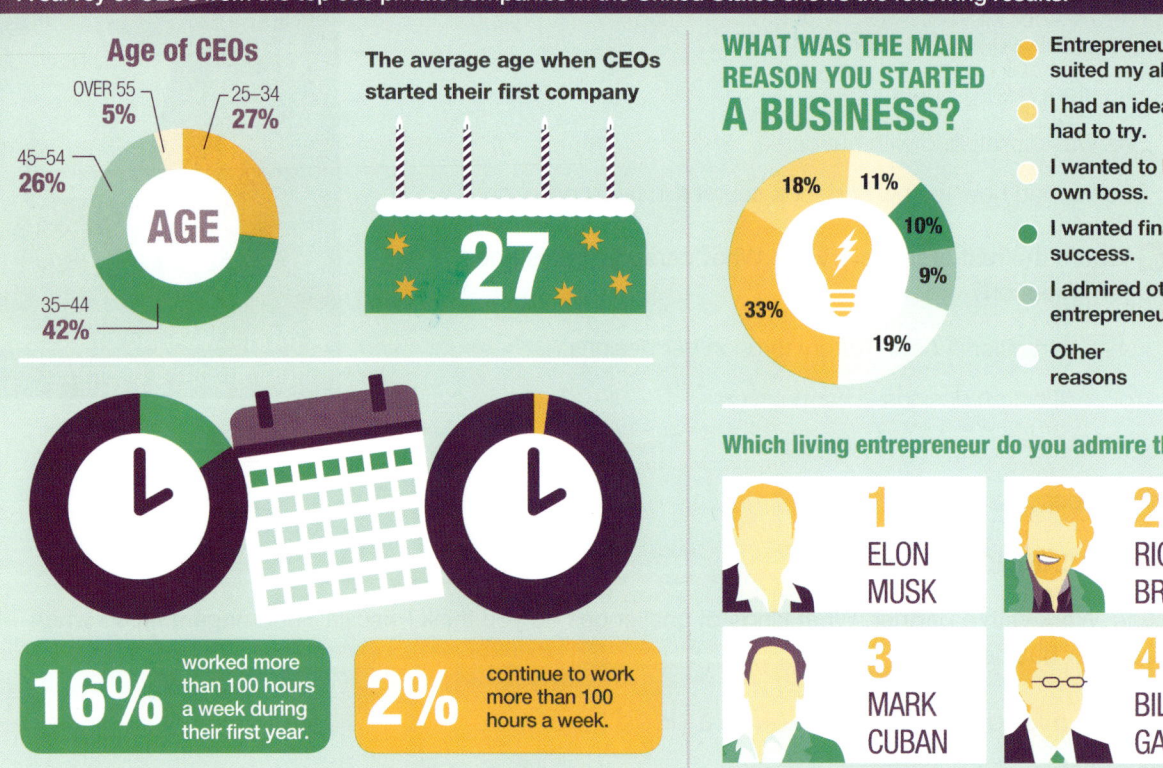

A survey of 500 CEOs

A survey of CEOs from the top 500 private companies in the United States shows the following results.

Age of CEOs
- OVER 55: 5%
- 25–34: 27%
- 45–54: 26%
- 35–44: 42%

The average age when CEOs started their first company: **27**

WHAT WAS THE MAIN REASON YOU STARTED A BUSINESS?
- 33% Entrepreneurship suited my abilities.
- 19% I had an idea I just had to try.
- 18% I wanted to be my own boss.
- 11% I wanted financial success.
- 10% I admired other entrepreneurs.
- 9% Other reasons

16% worked more than 100 hours a week during their first year.

2% continue to work more than 100 hours a week.

Which living entrepreneur do you admire the most?
1. ELON MUSK
2. RICHARD BRANSON
3. MARK CUBAN
4. BILL GATES

B ▶ **11.7** Watch an interview with Priscilla Shunmugam. What challenges did she face when she first started her business? Discuss with a partner.

C ▶ **11.8** Watch and study the language in the chart.

Talking about obligation and giving advice

The government *should* encourage people to support local businesses.
Leaders *have to* be good communicators.
Managers *need to* motivate their employees to do well.
I think companies *must* always plan ahead.

If you want to run a company, you *shouldn't* be afraid of making hard decisions.
People *don't have to* have a lot of experience in business to start their own company.
You *don't need to* be rich to be happy.
Even when things don't go according to plan, you *mustn't* give up.

For more information on **modals of necessity**, see Grammar Summary 11 on page 190.

D ▶ 11.7 Watch the interview in B again. Complete the sentences from the interview.

1 "So I _____ be my own supporter and my own critic, and make it work."

2 "I understand that we _____ make sacrifices for what we believe in. We _____ be brave and make hard decisions when needed."

3 "Opportunities don't always come along, so when you have one, you _____ grab it."

E Complete the sentences. Circle the correct words.

1 Leaders (**mustn't** / **don't have to**) know how to do everything, but they (**could** / **should**) be able to recruit the right people.

2 Businesses (**could** / **must**) be creative in order to attract more customers.

3 You (**couldn't** / **shouldn't**) just focus on the negative aspects of the job—there are lots of good points, too.

4 When you have a large and complicated project, you (**need to** / **don't need to**) break it down into small tasks.

F ▶ 11.9 Complete the information. Circle the correct words. Then listen and check your answers.

As the CEO of electric car company Tesla and rocket company SpaceX, Elon Musk is one of the world's most innovative business leaders. He believes that we [1] (**should** / **could**) create companies that tackle environment issues such as global warming. He also thinks that the price of oil [2] (**has to** / **doesn't have to**) be raised to discourage people from using it; instead, we [3] (**need to** / **mustn't**) use energy in a sustainable way.

Musk is already looking far into the future. He believes that humans may [4] (**have to** / **could**) live on other planets eventually. SpaceX aims to make it possible for us to travel to and live on Mars one day. The goals Musk has set aren't easy to achieve, but he is determined. "If something is important enough, even if the odds are against you, you [5] (**should** / **don't have to**) still do it," he says.

Elon Musk (right) speaking with a NASA employee

SPEAKING Interview with a CEO

A Work with a partner. You are going to do an interview. **Student A:** Read the information below. **Student B:** Turn to page 170.

> **Student A**
>
> You are the CEO of a small company. Think about your role: your company, what makes your company unique, your main goals, what you need to do, and the challenges you face. Note your ideas. A journalist will interview you.

B Conduct the interview. Take turns asking and answering the questions.

What are the future goals of your company?

We're working to make electric cars more popular.

11C Lessons in business

PRE-READING Scanning

Scan the first paragraph. How many businesses has Branson created over the course of his career?

Virgin Money's lounges function as community spaces. Local communities can request to use them for meetings or events at no cost.

▶ 11.10

1 The Virgin brand can be seen all over the world, offering almost every type of service or product imaginable—from mobile communication to travel to fitness. The founder of this global brand, Richard Branson, is no stranger to entrepreneurship. At 16, he started his first business, advertising records in a magazine called *Student*. From there, he went on to create Virgin Records, a successful chain of record stores. Fast-forward 50 years and 400 companies: Branson is one of the biggest names in business. To understand his success, it's worth taking a look at some of the business **principles** the self-made billionaire has followed as he built his empire.[1]

Branson is always **on the lookout** for ways a service or product could be improved; it doesn't matter if the industry is one he isn't familiar with. More importantly, his principle is only to go into a new industry when it is possible to give consumers something different. Virgin Money, for example, is unlike a traditional bank. Besides providing regular banking services, there are lounges for all customers. These lounges are designed like living rooms, where customers can watch TV, have a drink or snack, or borrow an iPad. The aim is to create a personal relationship with customers by making them feel comfortable.

Like most entrepreneurs, Branson isn't afraid of taking risks to expand his business. But he has had failures along the way. In 1994, Branson launched Virgin Cola in an attempt to compete with big companies such as Coca-Cola and Pepsi. However, Coca-Cola **took action** immediately—doubling the amount of money it spent on advertising. It was difficult to **win over** customers, and, in the end, Virgin Cola had to make a quiet exit. But Branson takes failures in his stride.[2] "Failure is a necessary part of business," he says, "so it's incredibly important for all entrepreneurs and business leaders to know when to call it a day,[3] learn from their mistakes, and move on, fast."

For Branson, life is about more than work; his number one rule is to have fun. As with his

144

businesses, he is completely committed to his
hobbies, such as adventure sports. Traveling on the Virgin Atlantic Flyer—the largest hot-air balloon ever made—he set two world records: one for being the first to cross the Atlantic Ocean, and another for crossing the Pacific.

Branson is also enthusiastic about charity work. He has **pledged** to give half his fortune away, and in 2004 he set up Virgin Unite, a nonprofit organization. Virgin Unite brings together people from all over the world to tackle a range of issues—from improving basic human rights to climate change—with the overall goal of making the world a better place.

So what is the secret? Richard Branson sums it up: "*Stuff* really is not what brings happiness. Family, friends, good health, and the satisfaction that comes from making a positive difference are what really matter."

[1] empire: *n.* a group of countries or businesses that are controlled by a single government or person
[2] take … in his stride: *v.* to accept something without being emotional
[3] call it a day: *v.* to stop doing something

UNDERSTANDING MAIN IDEAS

What principles do the following illustrate? Match.

1 Virgin Money   ○   ○   Be a force for good.
2 Virgin Cola   ○   ○   Recognize and learn from mistakes.
3 Virgin Atlantic Flyer   ○   ○   Differentiate yourself.
4 Virgin Unite   ○   ○   Enjoy what you do.

UNDERSTANDING DETAILS

Choose the correct options.

1 Virgin Records was Richard Branson's first _____.

   a business   b major failure   c major success

2 Virgin Money's lounges create _____ spaces for customers to relax in.

   a creative   b green   c informal

3 Virgin was unable to achieve success in the soft drink industry because _____.

   a it couldn't attract enough customers
   b customers found its product too expensive
   c customers complained about the taste of its drink

4 Which of these words best describes Richard Branson?

   a careful   b adventurous   c serious

BUILDING VOCABULARY

A Match the words in blue from the passage to the definitions.

1 principles   ○   ○   did something
2 on the lookout   ○   ○   rules or beliefs that influence behavior
3 took action   ○   ○   alert to
4 win over   ○   ○   promised to do something
5 pledged   ○   ○   succeed in getting someone's support

B Complete the sentences using the words in **A**.

1 Companies have to offer something innovative and different to _____ customers.
2 Government and business leaders have _____ to do what they can to limit global warming.
3 To become a trendsetter in an industry, you have to be _____ for new business ideas.

C **CRITICAL THINKING**

Inferring Work with a partner. What do you think Richard Branson means by "stuff"?

11D Life at 30,000 feet

TEDTALKS

Virgin founder **RICHARD BRANSON** owns a group of more than 400 companies. He has **dyslexia** and this made it more difficult for him to **grasp** concepts at school. However, by being **inquisitive** and open to challenges, Branson has managed to make his business a great success, effectively proving wrong any **stereotype** people might have of dyslexia.

Richard Branson's idea worth spreading is that succeeding in business means a lifetime of taking risks, failing, and picking yourself up again.

PREVIEWING

Read the paragraphs above. Match each **bold** word to its meaning. You will hear these words in the TED Talk.

1 understand   _____

2 curious   _____

3 a reading disorder _____

4 an idea of a person or thing that is usually untrue or overly simplified   _____

VIEWING

A ▶ **11.11** Watch Part 1 of the TED Talk. Answer questions 1 to 3.

1 According to Branson, what is the best way to run a company?

   a Learn from the best people in the industry.
   b Have a clear organizational structure and workflow process.
   c Hire the right people and inspire them to do well.

2 What does Branson mean when he says he loves to turn the status quo upside down?

   a He is easily bored with the way things are.
   b He tries something completely new or does things in a different way.
   c He thinks that office designs need to be unique.

3 How does Branson get ideas for new companies?

   a by researching the strategies of rival companies

   b by talking to people from various industries

   c by constantly thinking about how he could improve things

B ▶ 11.12 Watch Part 2 of the TED Talk. Which diagram below illustrates the analogy Branson describes?

C ▶ 11.13 Watch Part 3 of the TED Talk. Check (✓) the statements that best describe Richard Branson's business philosophy.

☐ It's important to build friendly relationships with other companies.

☐ Maintaining a good reputation is essential.

☐ You should keep track of your competitors' actions.

☐ Treat people well and in a fair way.

☐ Sometimes you have to be ruthless in business to succeed.

D CRITICAL THINKING

Evaluating Work with a partner. Which of Richard Branson's business principles do you think is the most surprising? Why?

> It's surprising that Branson's number one rule is to have fun. I always thought of CEOs as serious people.

> Yeah, I think CEOs really need to love what they do.

VOCABULARY IN CONTEXT

A ▶ 11.14 Watch the excerpts from the TED Talk. Choose the correct meaning of the words.

B Complete the sentences using the expressions in the box.

| give it a go | work it all out | draw out | knifing people in the back | take on |

1 Great leaders are able to _____ people's strengths and help them realize their potential.

2 Disagreements with your business partners are unavoidable, but when they happen, you should have a discussion to _____ .

3 Entrepreneurs usually have to be willing to _____ challenges.

4 You may be able to achieve success by _____ , but soon people won't want to work with you.

5 If you're really interested in something, you shouldn't be afraid to _____ .

PRESENTATION SKILLS Quoting people

> To make your presentation more interesting, you can quote what someone else has said when sharing a story or an example.

A ▶ 11.15 Watch part of Richard Branson's TED Talk. Choose the correct options.

1 Who did Branson quote?
  - **a** someone from his company
  - **b** a family member

2 What did he use the quote to describe?
  - **a** his business philosophy
  - **b** how he learned a business concept

B ▶ 11.16 Watch the excerpts from three other TED Talks. How do the speakers introduce the quotes? Complete the missing words.

1 The captain waved me over. _____, "Bezos, I need you to go into the house. I need you to go upstairs, past the fire, and I need you to get this woman a pair of shoes."

2 The people who lived there really hated it. _____, "What did you do? You painted our house in exactly the same color as the police station."

3 … the man to my right started telling me about all the ways that the Internet is degrading the English language. He brought up Facebook, and _____, "To defriend? I mean, is that even a real word?"

C Work with a partner. Look at the quotes in **B**. Why do you think the speakers chose to include the quotes?

11E Leadership roles

COMMUNICATE My business philosophy

A Decide your personal business style by ranking the descriptions in order of importance.

Values I look for in employees		My business philosophy	
quality of work	_____	Be different from others.	_____
work attitude	_____	Value your people.	_____
honesty	_____	Try to do good.	_____
innovation	_____	Try anything that interests you.	_____
ability to have fun	_____	Be ruthless when necessary.	_____

1 = most important, 5 = least important

B Work in groups. One group member is the retiring CEO, and the rest are potential successors. **Potential CEO successors:** Present your business philosophies and values to the CEO, and give reasons for your answers. **Retiring CEOs:** Listen to each candidate. Ask follow-up questions if needed.

> **Describing your business style**
>
> My idea of a good employee is …   I'd hire employees who …
> I want to build a business that focuses on …   My goal for the company is …

> I believe employees should have a good work attitude because …

> As far as I'm concerned, … is more important than … because …

C **Retiring CEOs:** Pick the candidate you think is the most convincing. This person will be the next CEO.

WRITING Describing your business style

Write about your business philosophy. Describe how you would run your company and what kinds of employees you would want if you were a business leader. Explain your ideas.

Inside the office of Tokopedia, one of Indonesia's biggest online shopping companies

> The way I would run a company would be to allow my employees to express their creativity and ideas. People are the most valuable resource in a company, so I think it's important to create an environment where they can do well. To do this, I would …

12 Well-being

"I learned the hard way the value of sleep."

Arianna Huffington
Co-founder of *The Huffington Post*, TED speaker

UNIT GOALS

In this unit, you will …

- talk about health and well-being.
- read about different ways to achieve work-life balance.
- watch a TED Talk about the importance of sleep.

WARM UP

▶ **12.1** Watch part of Arianna Huffington's TED Talk. Answer the questions with a partner.

1 The speaker is a famous businessperson. Why do you think she is giving a talk on sleep?

2 How do you feel when you don't get enough sleep?

A woman kickboxing in her home in Jeddah, Saudi Arabia

12A A healthy lifestyle

VOCABULARY Describing health and well-being

A ▶ **12.2** Complete the sentences using the words in the box. Then listen and check your answers.

| recharge | stressful | work-life balance | strengthen |

1 Losing a job is very _____.
2 Mental exercises, such as doing sudoku puzzles, can _____ your ability to solve problems.
3 Work shouldn't be everything in your life. It's equally important to engage in leisure activities and maintain a _____.
4 After a busy week at work, I often _____ on the weekend by doing something I enjoy.

B Complete the sentences. Circle the correct words.

1 A productive person is someone who works (**efficiently** / **confidently**) to produce good results.
2 To cope with a situation is to (**think about it** / **manage it well**).
3 To maintain a healthy diet, we have to (**build strong relationships** / **watch what we eat and drink**).
4 An active lifestyle involves (**a lot of exercise** / **going for medical checkups regularly**).

C Work with a partner. What is something you found stressful recently? How do you cope with difficult situations or challenges?

> The last time I experienced a stressful situation was when I gave a speech to the entire school.

> When I face a problem, I ask my friends for advice.

LISTENING What your brain does when you sleep

> **Listening for additional information**
> Words such as *which* and *that* introduce additional information to the main point of a sentence.

A ▶ **12.3** Watch an explanation of Jeffrey Iliff's research on sleep and the brain. What is the main point of the explanation?

   a Sleep is important because it's the only time for the brain to clear its waste.

   b We must sleep at the right time because the brain only clears its waste at certain times.

   c The amount of sleep each person needs varies according to how active the brain is during the day.

B ▶ **12.3** Watch again. Circle the correct words.

   1 The brain clears waste in a different way from the rest of the body because it (**has** / **lacks**) lymphatic vessels.

   2 Unlike the rest of the body, the brain is (**able** / **unable**) to clear its waste when we are awake.

   3 The brain switches to (**a cleaning** / **an inactive**) mode when we sleep.

Sleep studies help scientists find out what happens in our bodies when we sleep.

C CRITICAL THINKING

Inferring Work with a partner. What analogy does the speaker use? What is its purpose?

SPEAKING Talking about lifestyles

A ▶ **12.4** Why isn't Speaker B getting enough sleep?

   A: You've been yawning all day. Are you OK?

   B: Yeah. I'm just feeling tired.

   A: How much sleep did you get last night?

   B: About five hours, I guess.

   A: That's not enough. I heard we need about seven to nine hours of sleep every night.

   B: Yeah, I usually get more sleep. It's just that I've been stressed out over schoolwork recently.

   A: Maybe you should find a way to cope with the stress so you can get more rest. How about doing some exercise?

   B: I'm not really into sports. I prefer activities like reading.

   A: Reading is good, too. As long as it's something you enjoy, it will help reduce your stress.

B Practice the conversation with a partner.

C Work with a partner. Describe your lifestyle. Talk about your daily routines, interests, and how you take care of your health. Use the expressions in blue above to help you.

> I'm a morning person. I get up around seven every day to make breakfast.

> I can't get up that early. I prefer doing my work in the afternoon.

12B The importance of sleep

LANGUAGE FOCUS Discussing facts about sleep

A ▶ 12.5 Read the information. What time of the day are you usually most productive?

5 FACTS ABOUT SLEEP

Sleep plays an important role in our lives. A lack of sleep can affect our ability to work and study.

1 How many hours of sleep do we need each day?
- Newborns: 14–17
- Teenagers: 8–10
- Adults: 7–9
- Elderly adults: 7–8

2 Tiredness usually peaks twice a day, at 2 a.m. and 2 p.m.

3 If you fall asleep within 5 minutes, you're sleep deprived. The ideal time is between 10 and 15 minutes.

4 People can make terrible mistakes if they don't get enough sleep. Sleep deprivation played a role in accidents such as:
- the Exxon Valdez oil spill
- the Challenger space shuttle disaster
- the Chernobyl nuclear accident

5 Adult humans sleep about **3 hours less** than other primates. Chimps, monkeys, and baboons sleep around **10 hours** a day.

B ▶ 12.6 Listen to the conversation. What happens when we don't get enough sleep? How can getting enough sleep keep us healthy? Discuss with a partner.

C ▶ 12.7 Watch and study the language in the chart.

Talking about imaginary situations	
If I had more time after work, I'd hang out with my friends.	
If his house wasn't so far from the office, he'd bike to work every day.	
If I were you, I'd get advice from a fitness trainer.	'd = would
If she were rich, she'd travel around the world.	
If I lived by the sea, I'd go surfing every week.	
If there were more hours in a day, what would you do with the time?	

For more information on the **second conditional**, see Grammar Summary 12 on page 190.

D ▶ **12.6** Listen to the conversation in **B** again. Complete the sentences from the conversation.

1 "According to a study published in a medical journal, if you _____ for 24 hours, _____ as if you were drunk."

2 "If I _____ spend an hour commuting to work every day, _____ be able to get more sleep."

E Complete the sentences. Use the correct form of the words in parentheses.

1 According to a study, if everyone in the United States _____ (run) regularly, they _____ (lose) a total of almost one billion kilograms in weight.

2 A report by the United Nations estimates that if everyone in the world _____ (become) vegetarian, CO_2 emissions _____ (fall) by 17 percent.

3 If everyone _____ (drink) two liters of water a day, their skin _____ (look) much healthier.

4 If there _____ (be) more than 24 hours in a day, I _____ (spend) more time with my family.

5 If you _____ (can) go back in time, what changes _____ you _____ (make) to your lifestyle?

F Complete the sentences using your own ideas. Then share your ideas with a partner.

1 If I had to give up one type of food, _____ .

2 If I could be good at any sport, _____ .

3 I'd be much more productive at school if _____ .

The Colorado State University climbing team at a practice session

SPEAKING Describing your ideal lifestyle

Work with a partner. If you could plan your ideal lifestyle, what would it be like? Use the questions below to help you.

Where would you live? _____

What would your job be? _____

How many hours would you work a day? _____

What would you eat or drink every day? _____

What activities would you do every day? _____

I'd live in a house by the river and go fishing every day.

I'd run a small art gallery and spend my time painting.

12C Achieving work-life balance

PRE-READING Reflecting

Skim the first paragraph. How would you answer the opening question?

▶ 12.8

1   If you were given the **flexibility** to plan your day, what would it look like? Research has shown the benefits of a good work-life balance: reduced employee stress leading to better
5   performance and productivity, increased motivation and job **satisfaction**, and slower turnover[1] of staff.
    According to the Organization for Economic Co-operation and Development (OECD), workers in the Netherlands report the best work-life balance.
10 With only 0.4 percent of Dutch people working very long hours, nearly everybody has time for leisure activities. This is in contrast to Turkey, where four in ten people work over 50 hours a week.
    There isn't a clear **formula** for achieving work-
15 life balance. One way is perhaps to make a clear distinction between work and private life. In recent years, more and more companies in Sweden have **implemented** a six-hour workday. While at work, workers are encouraged to concentrate fully on work
20 and minimize distractions[2]—such as using social media and having long meetings. As a result, they have more time and energy to relax after they leave the office. Toyota service centers in Gothenburg, Sweden, switched to a six-hour workday in 2002.
25 Since then, the company has reported that their employees are happier, there is lower turnover, and it has become easier to recruit new staff.
    However, in reality, more people find themselves unable to enjoy their leisure time after long days at
30 work. Technology has made it possible for us to remain accessible all the time. In a recent study on work-life balance in the United States, almost half the employees surveyed said they feel **guilty** if they don't check in on work when out of the office.
35 So perhaps another way to promote work-life balance is to make work more enjoyable. Take Google for example: It makes its work environment fun, starting right from the design of its offices. No two Google offices look the same. But in every one,
40 there are kitchens filled with food and drink, fitness areas, shower rooms, gaming rooms, and places for employees to take naps.

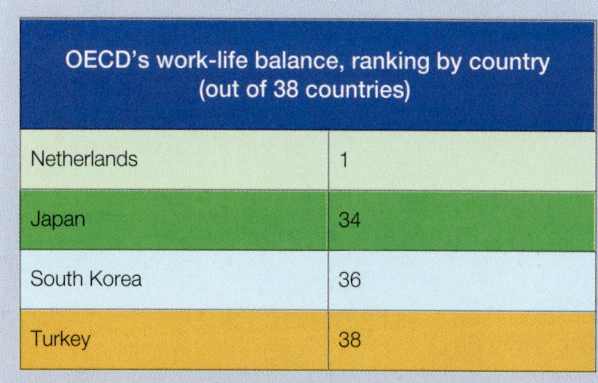

OECD's work-life balance, ranking by country (out of 38 countries)	
Netherlands	1
Japan	34
South Korea	36
Turkey	38

Percentage of people working long hours (>50 hours a week)

Netherlands 0.4 | OECD average 13 | Japan 22 | South Korea 23 | Turkey 39

A meeting area in the Google office in Dublin, Ireland

Employees are also able to plan their days flexibly. You can get into the office in the morning, do a workout in the middle of the day, return to work for a few hours, and maybe attend a workshop session. All of this is part of Google's efforts to improve employees' well-being and job satisfaction. Sandeep Chandna, a Google employee, believes that this approach is beneficial. "As long as it doesn't affect your work quality, you're basically free to plan how to spend your workday. I usually go for a run in the afternoon. If I get stuck on something, I take a quick break to play a game of ping-pong or foosball with my colleagues."

As people lead busier lives, moving away from a traditional work culture may be a way to achieve better work-life balance. And while there may be different ways of allowing people to enjoy both work and life, this certainly isn't an impossible goal.

[1] **turnover:** *n.* the rate at which the number of employees changes within the company
[2] **distractions:** *n.* things that take your attention away from a main task

UNDERSTANDING MAIN IDEAS

Choose the statement that best summarizes the main point of the passage.

a More companies should be like Google and create a pleasant workplace for their employees. This increases the well-being of their employees and makes them more productive.

b A work-life balance has clear benefits for both individuals and companies. It may not be easy to achieve, but there are a few possible approaches.

c Methods for achieving work-life balance differ from country to country. Governments need to understand how their people work in order to find the best way to keep them happy.

UNDERSTANDING DETAILS

Complete the concept map on work-life balance.

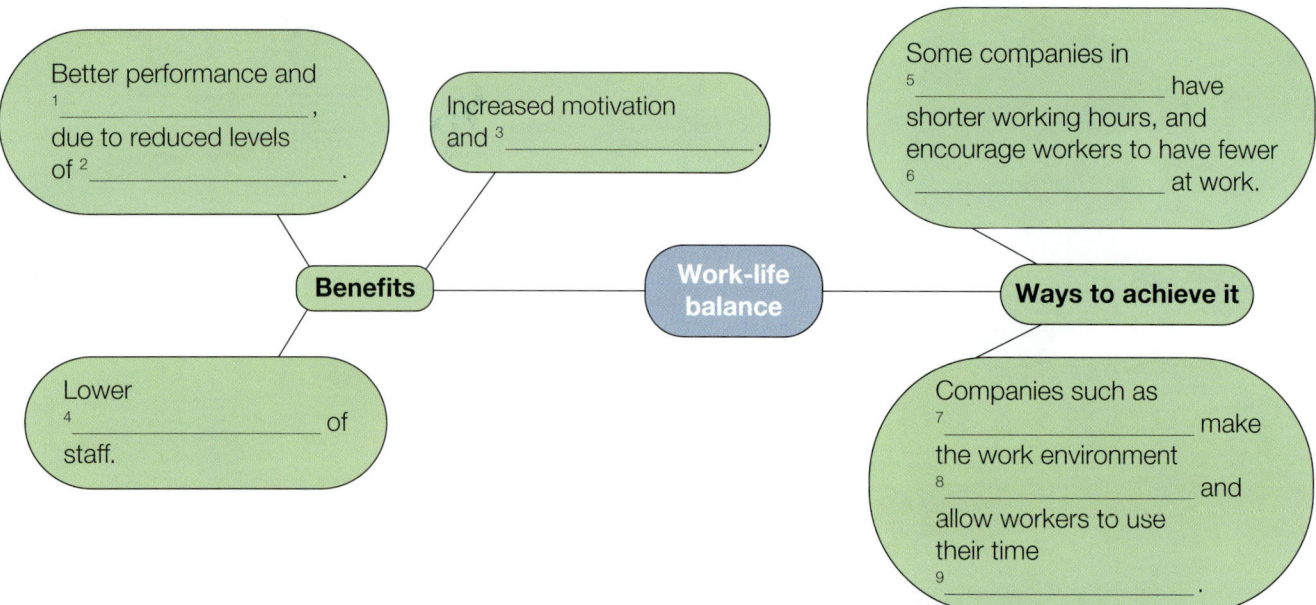

BUILDING VOCABULARY

A Complete the sentences using the words in blue from the passage.

1 A high level of job _____ makes employees feel more committed to their companies.

2 Companies today need to have the _____ to adapt to trends and changes.

3 I feel _____ whenever I'm unable to spend time with my family because of work.

4 There isn't a _____ for success in life—we need to put in the effort to achieve our goals.

5 Although a six-hour workday hasn't been _____ throughout Sweden, a number of Swedish companies are trying it out.

B CRITICAL THINKING

Evaluating Work with a partner. How would you describe the work-life balance situation in your country? Which of the two approaches mentioned in the article do you think you prefer?

> I think my country is slowly moving toward having better work-life balance because …

12D How to succeed? Get more sleep

TEDTALKS

ARIANNA HUFFINGTON is the co-founder and editor-in-chief of the popular online news site *The Huffington Post*. She is also a columnist and an author of more than ten books. Since 2007, she has encouraged people and businesses to create a balance between work and other parts of life.

Arianna Huffington's idea worth spreading is that a good night's sleep can lead to increased productivity and happiness—and smarter decision-making.

PREVIEWING

Read the paragraph below. Match each **bold** word to its meaning. You will hear these words in the TED Talk.

> Sleep is as important to our bodies as food and water. Being **deprived** of sleep can lead to negative consequences such as **exhaustion**. Yet people today are getting less sleep. Dr. Neil Kavey, director of the Sleep Disorder Center, believes our modern lifestyles may have resulted in a sleep deprivation **one-upmanship**. "Our society has valued people who **brag** about being able to function on very little sleep as a mark of someone who is aggressive, dynamic, successful," says Dr. Kavey. But he feels this isn't right. "Admire someone who puts focus on sleep and is not making mistakes (from sleep deprivation)," he suggests.

1 a state of extreme tiredness   _____
2 to speak in a boastful way   _____
3 without something you need   _____
4 trying to get an advantage over others _____

VIEWING

A ▶ **12.9** Watch Part 1 of the TED Talk. Answer questions 1 to 3.

1 Why does Arianna Huffington think that Type-A women are sleep-deprived?

   a They usually work better at night than in the day.
   b They tend to work too hard and sacrifice sleep.
   c They sometimes sacrifice sleep for leisure.

2 What words best describe how she used to be before she learned about the importance of sleep?

   a tired, overworked
   b full of energy, cheerful
   c busy, happy

3 According to Arianna Huffington, what are the benefits of getting more sleep?

   a a longer and more fulfilling life

   b a calmer and more peaceful life

   c a happier and more productive life

B ▶ 12.10 Watch Part 2 of the TED Talk. Check (✓) the main arguments that Arianna Huffington makes.

☐ Many people don't sleep enough because they think this makes them more productive.

☐ Lack of sleep is causing our leaders to make bad decisions.

☐ Studies show that women perform better at work because they get more rest than men.

☐ There are many leaders with high IQs but no innovative ideas.

☐ Technology can help us improve our quality of sleep.

☐ Getting enough sleep benefits both the individual and society.

C **CRITICAL THINKING**

Inferring Work with a partner. Discuss these questions.

1 Why does Arianna Huffington say that her idea can help unlock billions of big ideas?

2 What does Huffington mean when she says, "the essence of leadership is being able to see the iceberg before it hits the *Titanic*"? What is she comparing the *Titanic* and the iceberg to?

> Arianna Huffington is suggesting that …

> She feels that her idea can help people …

VOCABULARY IN CONTEXT

A ▶ 12.11 Watch the excerpts from the TED Talk. Choose the correct meaning of the words.

B Complete the sentences using the words in the box.

learning the hard way	hyper-connected	urged	the big picture

1 The fact that technology allows us to be _____ has both advantages and disadvantages.

2 Sometimes we become too focused on the everyday issues in our lives and fail to spend time looking at _____ and planning ahead.

3 For many years, medical experts have _____ people to have healthier lifestyles.

4 People who don't take care of their health may end up _____ when they fall sick.

PRESENTATION SKILLS Using humor

Sometimes, you can use humor as a way of connecting with your audience. Here are some points to note.

- Practice with someone. If the humor doesn't work, leave it out.
- Use humor carefully so that you don't offend your audience.
- Make sure that the joke illustrates the point you're making.

A ▶ 12.12 Watch part of Arianna Huffington's TED Talk. What point is she making with the jokes below? Choose the correct options.

1 a dinner with a man who had four hours of sleep

    a People who get enough sleep are more fun to be with.

    b People who don't get enough sleep become overly sensitive.

2 the collapse of the bank Lehman Brothers

    a Getting enough sleep gives you the ability to think more creatively.

    b Getting enough sleep helps you stay alert and focused.

B ▶ 12.13 Watch the excerpts from three other TED Talks. Why does the audience laugh in each case? Discuss with a partner.

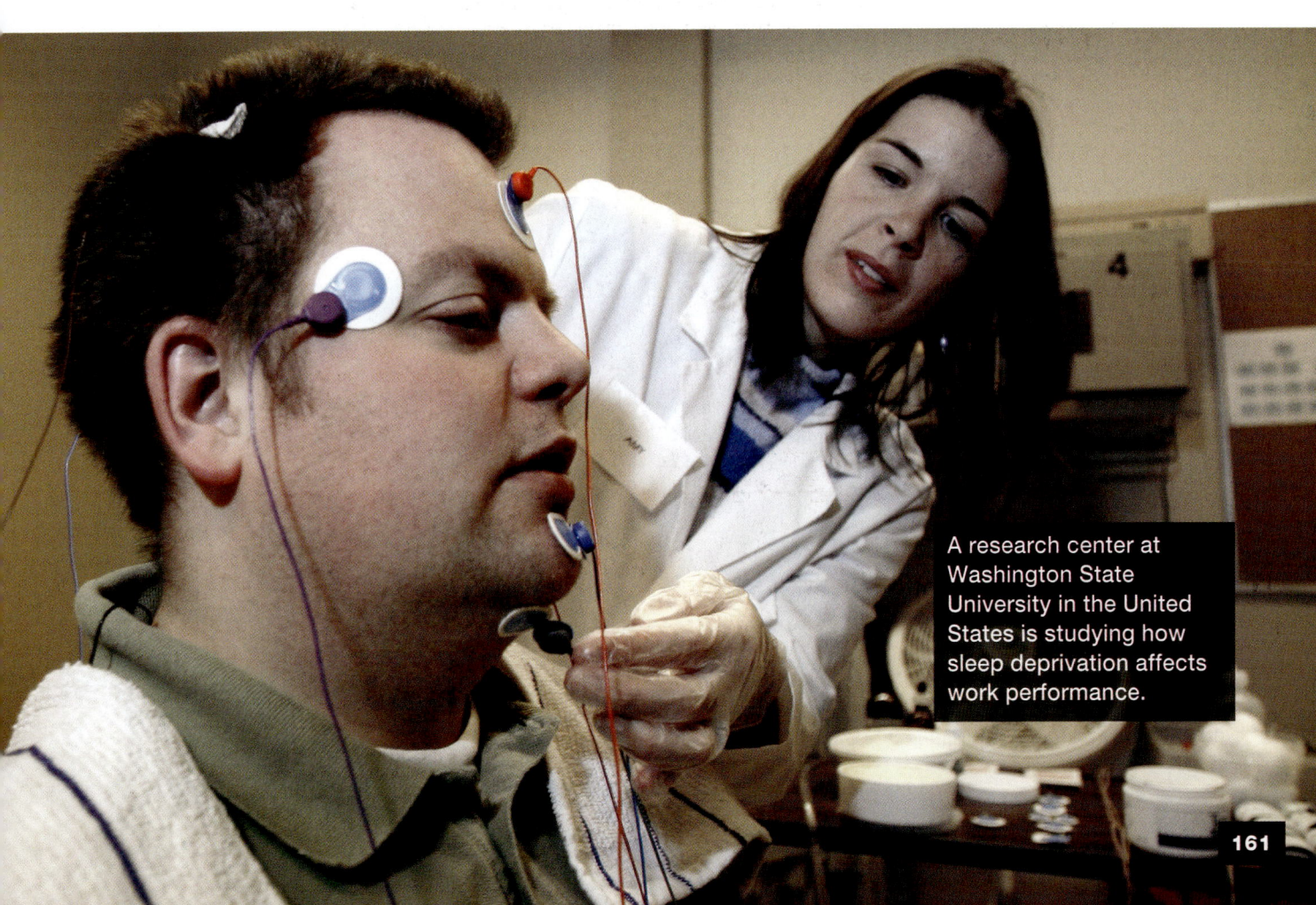

A research center at Washington State University in the United States is studying how sleep deprivation affects work performance.

12E Increasing productivity

COMMUNICATE Debate on work-life balance

A Work in two groups. Your school wants to increase the productivity of its students, and two suggestions have been made (see page 170). **Group A:** You are in favor of suggestion A. **Group B:** You are in favor of suggestion B.

B In your group, brainstorm the advantages of your suggestion and the disadvantages of the other suggestion. Make notes in the chart below.

Advantages	Disadvantages

C Have a debate on the topic with another group. Take turns explaining how your group's suggestion is better.

> **Making arguments**
> *The first point we'd like to raise is …*   *The other team claims that …*
> *To give an example of what we mean, …*   *It's important to note that …*

> My group believes that we should reduce the amount of time we spend at school …

> Although the idea of a shorter school day sounds attractive, we think that …

D Take a vote to decide on the approach the school should take.

WRITING Making suggestions

Write a few paragraphs about how you could improve your productivity at school or work. If you could make changes to your school or work, what kind of changes would you suggest?

> If I could, I'd like to be able to plan my own schedule at school. Personally, I find it easier to learn in the morning, so I'd plan my most important lessons at that time. Also, I'd …

The Florida International University campus in Miami

Presentation 4

MODEL PRESENTATION

A Complete the transcript of the presentation using the words in the box.

| productive | leave you with | satisfaction | career |
| recharge | according to | need to | had |

Hi, everybody. I'm Paul. Thanks for being here this morning. Do you know what the World Health Organization has called the health epidemic of the 21st century? ¹_____ studies, it affects one in three workers globally and costs societies billions of dollars. It's stress. Today, I want to suggest a way of reducing stress.

It's a well-known fact that stress over a long period of time can cause health problems such as heart disease and obesity. With increasing demands in the workplace and at home, it's no wonder that many people are experiencing stress. I believe we all ²_____ have greater work-life balance to counter stress. To do that, I'd like to propose the idea of a four-day workweek.

Think about it. First, if we all ³_____ three days off, we would have more time to focus on leisure activities and even go on short trips. We'd have more time to ⁴_____ and be with our family and friends. This helps strengthen our social relationships.

Research has shown that well-rested workers are more ⁵_____ and also better at problem solving. This increased job performance is likely to lead to greater overall job ⁶_____.

So, that's my suggestion to help people reduce their stress and lead happier, healthier lives. I'd like to ⁷_____ a quote by Hillary Clinton: "Don't confuse having a ⁸_____ with having a life." Thank you.

B ▶ P.4 Watch the presentation and check your answers.

C ▶ P.4 Review the list of presentation skills from Units 1–12 below. Which does the speaker use? Check (✓) them as you watch again. Then compare with a partner.

The speaker …
- helps the audience visualize by
  - using visuals ☐
- comments on visuals ☐
- opens with an interesting fact ☐
- asks the audience questions ☐
- ends with a hope for the future ☐
- engages with the audience ☐
- uses a story to personalize the message ☐
- uses signposting language ☐
- closes the loop ☐
- gives a demonstration ☐
- quotes someone ☐
- uses humor ☐

YOUR TURN

A You are going to plan and give a short persuasive presentation about a way to achieve a better work-life balance. Give your opinion and explain your reasons. Make notes in the chart below.

Suggestion for a better work-life balance
Reasons

B Look at the useful phrases in the box below. Think about which ones you will need in your presentation.

> **Useful phrases**
>
> **Describing scenarios:** *If we could …, it would …*
> *Imagine if we were …*
>
> **Supporting your argument:** *Studies suggest/show that …*
> *According to research by …*
>
> **Using a quote:** *As … says, …*
> *I'll leave you with a quote by …*

C Work with a partner. Take turns giving your presentation using your notes. Use some of the presentation skills from Units 1–12. As you listen, check (✓) each skill your partner uses.

The speaker …
- helps the audience visualize by
  - using visuals ☐
- comments on visuals ☐
- opens with an interesting fact ☐
- asks the audience questions ☐
- ends with a hope for the future ☐
- engages with the audience ☐
- uses a story to personalize the message ☐
- uses signposting language ☐
- closes the loop ☐
- gives a demonstration ☐
- quotes someone ☐
- uses humor ☐

D Give your partner some feedback on their talk. Include at least two things you liked and one thing that could be improved.

> That was a wonderful presentation. You were engaging and humorous. But you need to use clearer signposting language to organize your talk.

Communication Activities

2E COMMUNICATE

STUDENT A

Read the information below. Then explain to your partner what the innovation is.

Food-scanning technology

What it is

This technology allows you to use devices called food scanners to check the nutritional details of the food you're eating.

How it works

The device scans food and analyzes its chemical breakdown. It then sends detailed information about the food item, such as the amount of calories, proteins, or fat, to an app on your smartphone.

How this changes things

- People don't have to spend time examining food labels to find out if the food contains anything they can't eat or don't want to eat.
- People can keep track of what they eat more accurately.

3B SPEAKING

STUDENT A

Read the information below. Make notes or highlight key words. Then describe the technology to your partner and explain the effects it could have on people in the future.

Sensors that you can eat

What are they?

These are small monitoring devices in the form of medicine pills. Once eaten, these devices monitor your body and send information wirelessly to your smartphone or computer.

Examples of potential benefits

- Patients can easily monitor their health.
- Doctors could use the data to decide on the most suitable treatment for a patient. Patients don't have to visit the hospital for physical checkups.
- Medical researchers could gather data on patients with similar health conditions or illnesses to find cures.

> As edible sensors are able to constantly monitor your health, doctors can …

2E COMMUNICATE

STUDENT B

Read the information below. Then explain to your partner what the innovation is.

Mobile payment technology

What it is

This technology allows you to use mobile phones to pay for all kinds of things.

How it works

Users create an account on an app on their smartphones. They then store their credit card details in the app.

How this changes things

- People won't have to carry around bulky wallets or worry about forgetting to take their loyalty/rewards card with them.
- It will be easier to split payments when you're eating or shopping with a group of people.
- Shops can use the data from mobile payments to offer customers personalized deals.

3B SPEAKING

STUDENT B

Read the information below. Make notes or highlight key words. Then describe the technology to your partner and explain the effects it could have on people in the future.

3-D printers for body parts

What are they?

These are machines that can print various parts of our body such as skin, bone, or organs. 3-D printers already exist, but they are not yet being widely used for healthcare purposes.

Examples of potential benefits

- Patients who need organ donations don't have to wait for suitable donors.
- Patients with burns or skin diseases can replace the affected areas with new skin.
- We could create new bones for people suffering from bone-related diseases or who have serious injuries.

> 3-D printers are very useful for healthcare because they may be able to quickly produce …

9B SPEAKING

STUDENT A

Look at the chart below. Tell your partner about what the words in column A used to mean. Ask your partner about the words in column B.

A	B
clue (n.) Hundreds of years ago, a clue used to mean "a ball of thread" or "a ball of string."	**bully (n.)** In the 16th century, this word meant "darling" or "sweetheart." In the 17th century, the word meant "_____."
guy (n.) Hundreds of years ago, this word used to mean "a terrible or awful man."	**husband (n.)** Up until 600 or 700 years ago, this word used to refer to the _____.
nervous (adj.) About 500 or 600 years ago, the word used to mean "strong and full of energy."	**meat (n.)** This word used to refer to _____ in general, rather than the flesh of _____.

9E COMMUNICATE

GROUP A

Think of two incorrect definitions for each word or phrase below. Write them in the chart.

Word/phrase	Meaning	Example sentence
on fleek (adj.)	**Real meaning:** perfect, stylish **Incorrect meanings:**	She looks on fleek today.
have no chill (v.)	**Real meaning:** to overreact unnecessarily **Incorrect meanings:**	My friend has no chill—she's always worrying about unimportant things.
flex (v.)	**Real meaning:** to show off, often with money **Incorrect meanings:**	He's been flexing ever since he bought a new sports car.

4B SPEAKING

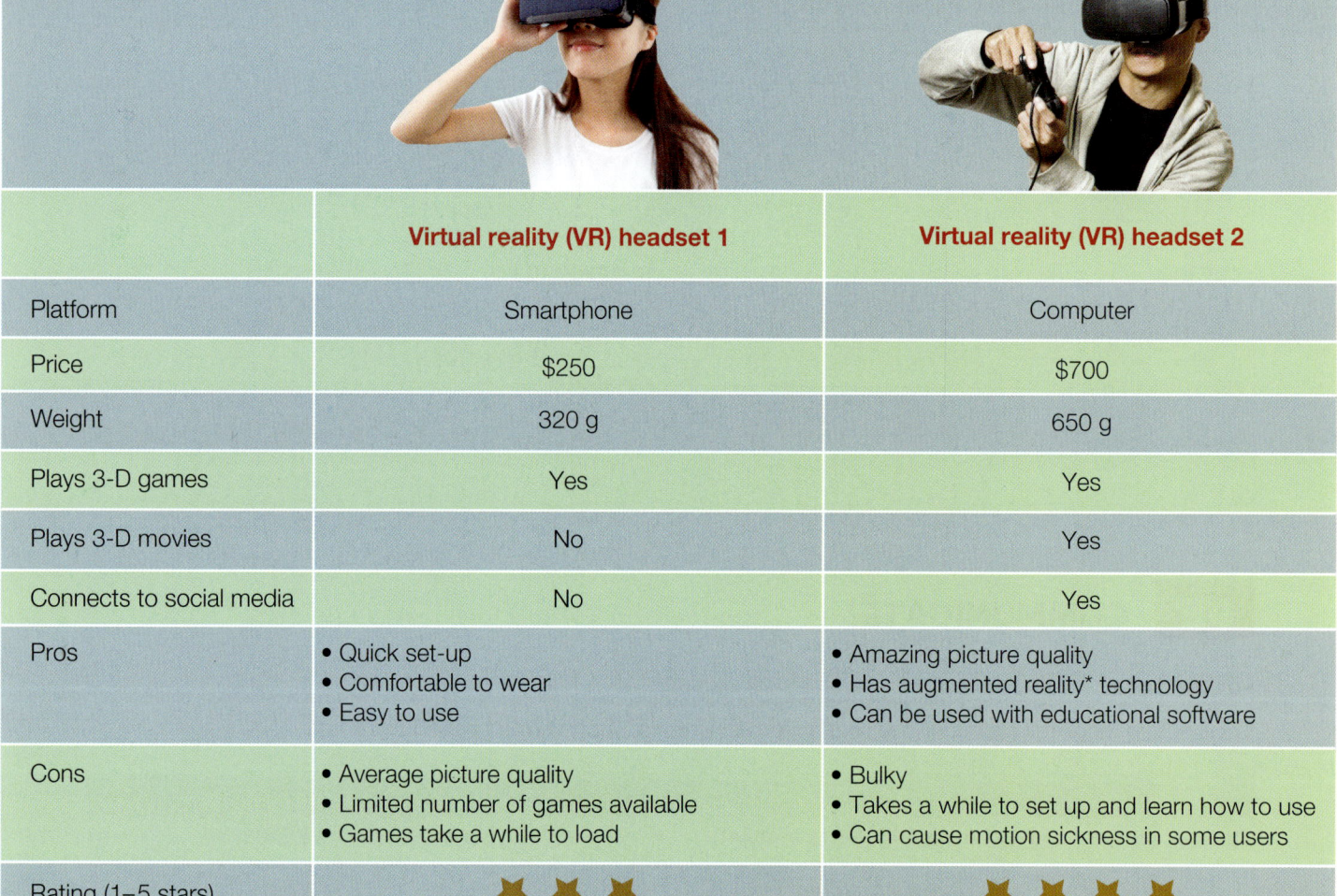

	Virtual reality (VR) headset 1	Virtual reality (VR) headset 2
Platform	Smartphone	Computer
Price	$250	$700
Weight	320 g	650 g
Plays 3-D games	Yes	Yes
Plays 3-D movies	No	Yes
Connects to social media	No	Yes
Pros	• Quick set-up • Comfortable to wear • Easy to use	• Amazing picture quality • Has augmented reality* technology • Can be used with educational software
Cons	• Average picture quality • Limited number of games available • Games take a while to load	• Bulky • Takes a while to set up and learn how to use • Can cause motion sickness in some users
Rating (1–5 stars)	★★★	★★★★

*__Augmented reality:__ You see both the virtual world and the real world through the headset. You are able to interact with virtual contents in the real world, and distinguish between the two.

9B SPEAKING

STUDENT B

Look at the chart below. Ask your partner about the words in column A. Tell your partner about what the words in column B used to mean.

A	B
clue (n.) Hundreds of years ago, a clue used to mean "a ball of _____" or "a ball of _____."	**bully (n.)** In the 16th century, this word meant "darling" or "sweetheart." In the 17th century, the word meant "a good person."
guy (n.) Hundreds of years ago, this word used to mean "a _____ man."	**husband (n.)** Up until 600 or 700 years ago, this word used to refer to the owner of a house.
nervous (adj.) About 500 or 600 years ago, the word used to mean "strong and _____."	**meat (n.)** This word used to refer to food in general, rather than the flesh of animals.

9E COMMUNICATE

GROUP B

Think of two incorrect definitions for each word or phrase below. Write them in the chart.

Word/phrase	Meaning	Example sentence
black elephant (n.)	**Real meaning:** an unlikely high-risk event that everyone knows about but avoids discussing **Incorrect meanings:**	The issue of global warming is a black elephant.
dad bod (n.)	**Real meaning:** a slightly plump male body, usually considered attractive **Incorrect meanings:**	He is starting to develop a dad bod.
mathwash (v.)	**Real meaning:** to make a topic seem objective by using mathematics or logic **Incorrect meanings:**	Some companies mathwash customers when selling their products.

11B SPEAKING

STUDENT B

You are a journalist who is going to interview the CEO of a small company. Think of some questions to ask. Here are some ideas:
- What are your main goals?
- What do you have to do in order to achieve those goals?
- What advice would you give to people who want to start their business?

12E COMMUNICATE

SUGGESTION A

We want to reduce the amount of time students spend at school. During school hours, students will not be allowed to use their personal cell phones and other electronic devices—they will focus on their studies. Break time will also be reduced. With a short school day, students will have more time to explore their interests or work on projects after school.

SUGGESTION B

We want to allow more flexibility in learning. Students will be able to plan the sequence of the lessons they have for each day. They won't always have to be in class for lessons. Instead, they will choose to join lessons online, at any place and time throughout the school day. Students will have time between lessons to engage in non-academic activities.

6B LANGUAGE FOCUS

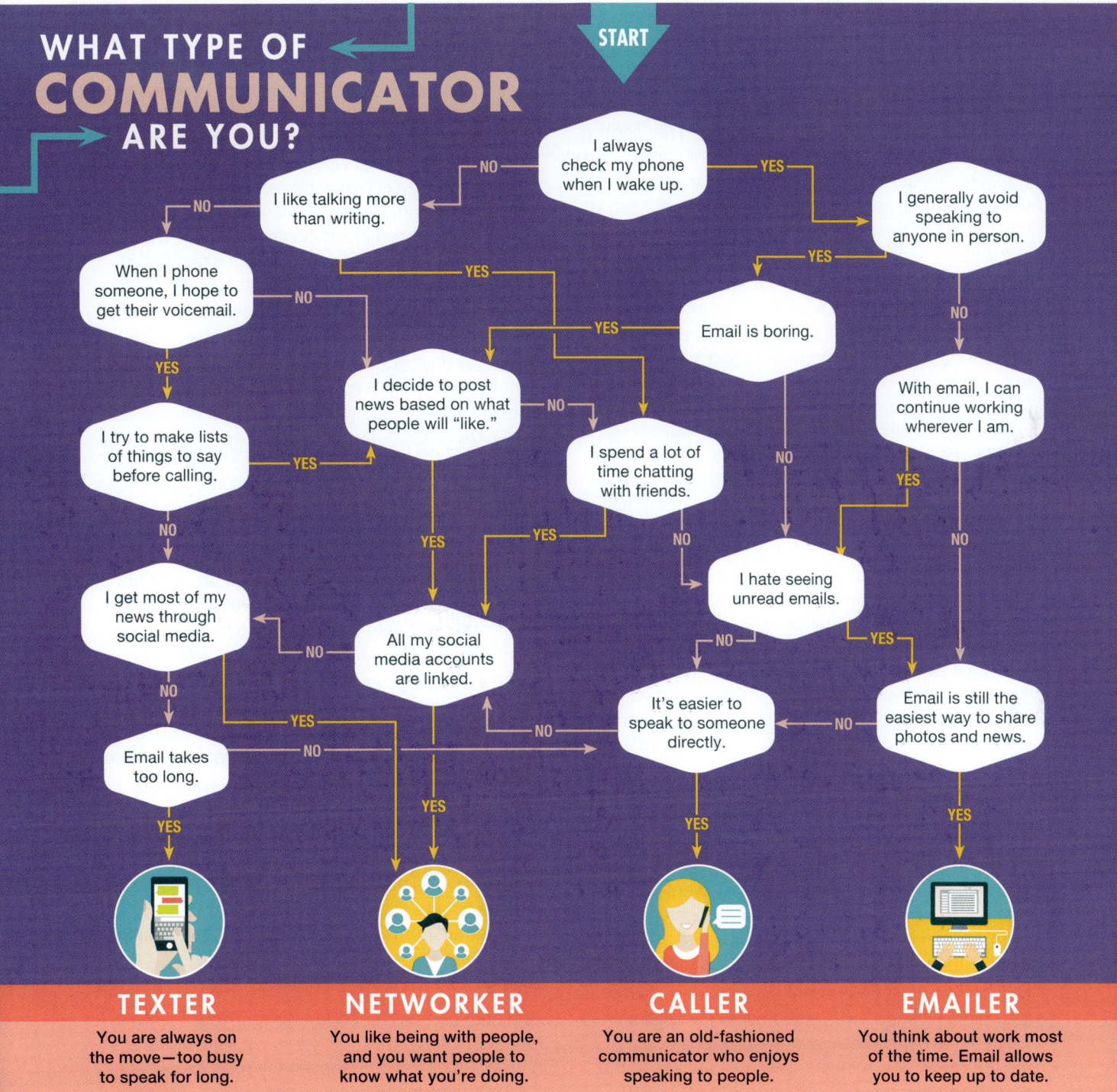

TED Talk Transcripts

Unit 1 Mark Bezos: A life lesson from a volunteer firefighter

Part 1

Back in New York, I am the head of development for a non-profit called Robin Hood. When I'm not fighting poverty, I'm fighting fires as the assistant captain of a volunteer fire company. Now in our town, where the volunteers supplement a highly skilled career staff, you have to get to the fire scene pretty early to get in on any action.

I remember my first fire. I was the second volunteer on the scene, so there was a pretty good chance I was going to get in. But still it was a real footrace against the other volunteers to get to the captain in charge to find out what our assignments would be. When I found the captain, he was having a very engaging conversation with the homeowner, who was surely having one of the worst days of her life. Here it was, the middle of the night, she was standing outside in the pouring rain, under an umbrella, in her pajamas, barefoot, while her house was in flames.

Part 2

The other volunteer who had arrived just before me—let's call him Lex Luthor—(Laughter) got to the captain first and was asked to go inside and save the homeowner's dog. The dog! I was stunned with jealousy. Here was some lawyer or money manager who, for the rest of his life, gets to tell people that he went into a burning building to save a living creature, just because he beat me by five seconds. Well, I was next. The captain waved me over. He said, "Bezos, I need you to go into the house. I need you to go upstairs, past the fire, and I need you to get this woman a pair of shoes." (Laughter) I swear. So, not exactly what I was hoping for, but off I went—up the stairs, down the hall, past the "real" firefighters, who were pretty much done putting out the fire at this point, into the master bedroom to get a pair of shoes.

Now I know what you're thinking, but I'm no hero. (Laughter) I carried my payload back downstairs where I met my nemesis and the precious dog by the front door. We took our treasures outside to the homeowner, where, not surprisingly, his received much more attention than did mine. A few weeks later, the department received a letter from the homeowner thanking us for the valiant effort displayed in saving her home. The act of kindness she noted above all others: someone had even gotten her a pair of shoes.

(Laughter)

Part 3

In both my vocation at Robin Hood and my avocation as a volunteer firefighter, I am witness to acts of generosity and kindness on a monumental scale, but I'm also witness to acts of grace and courage on an individual basis. And you know what I've learned? They all matter. So as I look around this room at people who either have achieved, or are on their way to achieving, remarkable levels of success, I would offer this reminder: don't wait. Don't wait until you make your first million to make a difference in somebody's life. If you have something to give, give it now. Serve food at a soup kitchen. Clean up a neighborhood park. Be a mentor.

Not every day is going to offer us a chance to save somebody's life, but every day offers us an opportunity to affect one. So get in the game. Save the shoes.

Thank you.

Unit 2 Derek Sivers: How to start a movement

Part 1

So, ladies and gentlemen, at TED we talk a lot about leadership and how to make a movement. So let's watch a movement happen, start to finish, in under three minutes and dissect some lessons from it.

First, of course you know, a leader needs the guts to stand out and be ridiculed. But what he's doing is so easy to follow. So here's his first follower with a crucial role; he's going to show everyone else how to follow.

Now, notice that the leader embraces him as an equal. So, now it's not about the leader anymore; it's about them, plural. Now, there he is calling to his friends. Now, if you notice that the first follower is actually an underestimated form of leadership in itself. It takes guts to stand out like that. The first follower is what transforms a lone nut into a leader. (Laughter) (Applause)

Part 2

And here comes a second follower. Now it's not a lone nut, it's not two nuts—three is a crowd, and a crowd is news. So a movement must be public. It's important to show not just the leader, but the followers, because you find that new followers emulate the followers, not the leader.

Now, here come two more people, and immediately after, three more people. Now we've got momentum. This is the tipping point. Now we've got a movement. So, notice that, as more people join in, it's less risky.

So those that were sitting on the fence before, now have no reason not to. They won't stand out, they won't be ridiculed, but they will be part of the in-crowd if they hurry. (Laughter) So, over the next minute, you'll see all of those that prefer to stick with the crowd because eventually they would be ridiculed for not joining in. And that's how you make a movement.

Part 3

But let's recap some lessons from this. So first, if you are the type, like the shirtless dancing guy that is standing alone, remember the importance of nurturing your first few followers as equals so it's clearly about the movement, not you. OK, but we might have missed the real lesson here.

The biggest lesson, if you noticed—did you catch it?—is that leadership is over-glorified. That, yes, it was the shirtless guy who was first, and he'll get all the credit, but it was really the first follower that transformed the lone nut into a leader. So, as we're told that we should all be leaders, that would be really ineffective.

If you really care about starting a movement, have the courage to follow and show others how to follow. And when you find a lone nut doing something great, have the guts to be the first one to stand up and join in. And what a perfect place to do that, at TED.

Thanks. (Applause)

Unit 3 Kenneth Shinozuka: My simple invention, designed to keep my grandfather safe

Part 1

What's the fastest growing threat to Americans' health? Cancer? Heart attacks? Diabetes? The answer is actually none of these; it's Alzheimer's disease. Every 67 seconds, someone in the United States is diagnosed with Alzheimer's. As the number of Alzheimer's patients triples by the year 2050, caring for them, as well as the rest of the aging population, will become an overwhelming societal challenge.

My family has experienced firsthand the struggles of caring for an Alzheimer's patient. Growing up in a family with three generations, I've always been very close to my grandfather. When I was four years old, my grandfather and I were walking in a park in Japan when he suddenly got lost. It was one of the scariest moments I've ever experienced in my life, and it was also the first instance that informed us that my grandfather had Alzheimer's disease. Over the past 12 years, his condition got worse and worse, and his wandering in particular caused my family a lot of stress. My aunt, his primary caregiver, really struggled to stay awake at night to keep an eye on him, and even then often failed to catch him leaving the bed. I became really concerned about my aunt's well-being as well as my grandfather's safety. I searched extensively for a solution that could help my family's problems, but couldn't find one.

Part 2

Then, one night about two years ago, I was looking after my grandfather and I saw him stepping out of the bed. The moment his foot landed on the floor, I thought, why don't I put a pressure sensor on the heel of his foot? Once he stepped onto the floor and out of the bed, the pressure sensor would detect an increase in pressure caused by body weight and then wirelessly send an audible alert to the caregiver's smartphone. That way, my aunt could sleep much better at night without having to worry about my grandfather's wandering.

So now I'd like to perform a demonstration of the sock. Could I please have my sock model on stage? Great. So once the patient steps onto the floor—(Ringing)—an alert is sent to the caregiver's smartphone.

Thank you. (Applause)

Thank you, sock model.

So this is a drawing of my preliminary design.

My desire to create a sensor-based technology perhaps stemmed from my lifelong love for sensors and technology. When I was six years old, an elderly family friend fell down in the bathroom and suffered severe injuries. I became concerned about my own grandparents and decided to invent a smart bathroom system. Motion sensors would be installed inside the tiles of bathroom floors to detect the falls of elderly patients whenever they fell down in the bathroom. Since I was only six years old at the time and I hadn't graduated from kindergarten yet, I didn't have the necessary resources and tools to translate my idea into reality, but nonetheless, my research experience really implanted in me a firm desire to use sensors to help the elderly people. I really believe that sensors can improve the quality of life of the elderly.

Part 3

[. . .] I've tested the device on my grandfather for about a year now, and it's had a 100 percent success rate in detecting the over 900 known cases of his wandering. Last summer, I was able to beta test my device at several residential care facilities in California, and I'm currently incorporating the feedback to further improve the device into a marketable product. Testing the device on a number of patients made me realize that I needed to invent solutions for people who didn't want to wear socks to sleep at night.

So sensor data, collected on a vast number of patients, can be useful for improving patient care and also leading to a cure for the disease, possibly. For example, I'm currently examining correlations between the frequency of a patient's nightly wandering and his or her daily activities and diet.

One thing I'll never forget is when my device first caught my grandfather's wandering out of bed at night. At that moment, I was really struck by the power of technology to change lives for the better. People living happily and healthily—that's the world that I imagine.

Thank you very much.

(Applause)

Unit 4 Margaret Gould Stewart: How giant websites design for you (and a billion others, too)

Part 1

What do you think of when I say the word "design"? You probably think of things like this: finely crafted objects that you can hold in your hand, or maybe logos and posters and maps that visually explain things, classic icons of timeless design. But I'm not here to talk about that kind of design. I want to talk about the kind that you probably use every day and may not give much thought to, designs that change all the time and that live inside your pocket. I'm talking about the design of digital experiences and specifically the design of systems that are so big that their scale can be hard to comprehend. Consider the fact that Google processes over one billion search queries every day, that every minute, over 100 hours of footage are uploaded to YouTube. That's more in a single day than all three major U.S. networks broadcast in the last five years combined. And Facebook transmitting the photos, messages, and stories of over 1.23 billion people. That's almost half of the Internet population, and a sixth of humanity.

These are some of the products that I've helped design over the course of my career, and their scale is so massive that they've produced unprecedented design challenges. But what is really hard about designing at scale is this: It's hard in part because it requires a combination of two things, audacity and humility—audacity to believe that the thing that you're making is something that the entire world wants and needs, and humility to understand that as a designer, it's not about you or your portfolio, it's about the people that you're designing for, and how your work just might help them live better lives. Now, unfortunately, there's no school that offers the course Designing for Humanity 101. I and the other designers who work on these kinds of products have had to kind of invent it as we go along, and we are teaching ourselves the emerging best practices of designing at scale, and today I'd like to share some of the things that we've learned over the years.

Part 2

Now, the first thing that you need to know about designing at scale is that the little things really matter. Here's a really good example of how a very tiny design element can make a big impact. Now, the team at Facebook that manages the Facebook "Like" button decided that it needed to be redesigned. The button had kind of gotten out of sync with the evolution of our brand and it needed to be modernized. Now you might think, well, it's a tiny little button, it probably is a pretty straightforward, easy design assignment, but it wasn't. Turns out, there were all kinds of constraints for the design of this button. You had to work within specific height and width parameters. You had to be careful to make it work in a bunch of different languages, and be careful about using fancy gradients or borders because it has to degrade gracefully in old web browsers. The truth is, designing this tiny little button was a huge pain in the butt.

Now, this is the new version of the button, and the designer who led this project estimates that he spent over 280 hours redesigning this button over the course of months. Now, why would we spend so much time on something so small? It's because when you're designing at scale, there's no such thing as a small detail. This innocent little button is seen on average 22 billion times a day and on over 7.5 million websites. It's one of the single most viewed design elements ever created. Now that's a lot of pressure for a little button and the designer behind it, but with these kinds of products, you need to get even the tiny things right.

Part 3

[. . .] Now, when you set a goal to design for the entire human race, and you start to engage in that goal in earnest, at some point you run into the walls of the bubble that you're living in. Now, in San Francisco, we get a little miffed when we hit a dead cell zone because we can't use our phones to navigate to the new hipster coffee shop. But what if you had to drive four hours to charge your phone because you had no reliable source of electricity? What if you had no access to public libraries? What if your country had no free press? What would these products start to mean to you? This is what Google, YouTube, and Facebook look like to most of the world, and it's what they'll look like to most of the next five billion people to come online. Designing for low-end cell phones is not glamorous design work, but if you want to design for the whole world, you have to design for where people are, and not where you are.

So how do we keep this big, big picture in mind? We try to travel outside of our bubble to see, hear, and understand the people we're designing for. We use our products in non-English languages to make sure that they work just as well. And we try to use one of these phones from time to time to keep in touch with their reality.

So what does it mean to design at a global scale? It means difficult and sometimes exasperating work to try to improve and evolve products. Finding the audacity and the humility to do right by them can be pretty exhausting, and the humility part, it's a little tough on the design ego. Because these products are always changing, everything that I've designed in my career is pretty much gone, and everything that I will design will fade away. But here's what remains: the never-ending thrill of being a part of something that is so big, you can hardly get your head around it, and the promise that it just might change the world.

Thank you.

(Applause)

Unit 5 Haas and Hahn: How painting can transform communities

Part 1

Dre Urhahn: This theater is built on Copacabana, which is the most famous beach in the world. But 25 kilometers away from here in the North Zone of Rio lies a community called Vila Cruzeiro, and roughly 60,000 people live there. Now, the people here in Rio mostly know Vila Cruzeiro from the news, and unfortunately, news from Vila Cruzeiro often is not good news. But Vila Cruzeiro is also the place where our story begins.

Jeroen Koolhaas: Ten years ago, we first came to Rio to shoot a documentary about life in the favelas. Now, we learned that favelas are informal communities. They emerged over the years when immigrants from the countryside came to the cities looking for work, like cities within the cities, known for problems with crime, poverty, and the violent drug war between police and the drug gangs. So what struck us was that these were communities that the people who lived there had built with their own hands, without a master plan and like a giant work in progress. Where we're from, in Holland, everything is planned. We even have rules for how to follow the rules. (Laughter)

DU: So the last day of filming, we ended up in Vila Cruzeiro, and we were sitting down and we had a drink, and we were overlooking this hill with all these houses, and most of these houses looked unfinished, and they had walls of bare brick, but we saw some of these houses that were plastered and painted, and suddenly we had this idea: what would it look like if all these houses would be plastered and painted? And then we imagined one big design, one big work of art. Who would expect something like that in a place like this? So we thought, would that even be possible?

Part 2

[. . .] JK: We had a friend. He ran an NGO in Vila Cruzeiro. His name was Nanko, and he also liked the idea. He said, "You know, everybody here would pretty much love to have their houses plastered and painted. It's when a house is finished." So he introduced us to the right people, and Vitor and Maurinho became our crew. We picked three houses in the center of the community and we start here. We made a few designs, and everybody liked this design of a boy flying a kite the best. So we started painting, and the first thing we did was to paint everything blue, and we thought that looked already pretty good. But they hated it. The people who lived there really hated it. They said, "What did you do? You painted our house in exactly the same color as the police station." (Laughter) In a favela, that is not a good thing. Also the same color as the prison cell. So we quickly went ahead and we painted the boy, and then we thought we were finished, we were really happy, but still, it wasn't good because the little kids started coming up to us, and they said, "You know, there's a boy flying the kite, but where is his kite?" We said, "Uh, it's art. You know, you have to imagine the kite." (Laughter) And they said, "No, no, no, we want to see the kite." So we quickly installed a kite way up high on the hill, so that you could see the boy flying the kite and you could actually see a kite. So the local news started writing about it, which was great, and then even The Guardian wrote about it: "Notorious slum becomes open-air gallery."

Part 3

[. . .] DU: So then we received an unexpected phone call from the Philadelphia Mural Arts Program, and they had this question if this idea, our approach, if this would actually work in North Philly, which is one of the poorest neighborhoods in the United States. So we immediately said yes. We had no idea how, but it seemed like a very interesting challenge, so we did exactly the same as we did in Rio, and we moved into the neighborhood and started barbecuing. (Laughter) So the project took almost two years to complete, and we made individual designs for every single house on the avenue that we painted, and we made these designs together with the local store owners, the building owners, and a team of about a dozen young men and women. They were hired, and then they were trained as painters, and together they transformed their own neighborhood, the whole street, into a giant patchwork of color. (Applause) And at the end, the city of Philadelphia thanked every single one of them and gave them like a merit for their accomplishment.

[. . .] DU: So while this is happening, we are bringing this idea all over the world. So, like the project we did in Philadelphia, we are also invited to do workshops, for instance in Curaçao, and right now we're planning a huge project in Haiti.

JK: So the favela was not only the place where this idea started: it was also the place that made it possible to work without a master plan, because these communities are informal—this was the inspiration— and in a communal effort, together with the people, you can almost work like in an orchestra, where you have a hundred instruments playing together to create a symphony.

DU: So we want to thank everybody who wanted to become part of this dream and supported us along the way, and we are looking at continuing.

JK: Yeah. And so one day pretty soon, when the colors start going up on these walls, we hope more people will join us, and, you know, join this big dream, and so that maybe one day, the whole of Vila Cruzeiro will be painted.

DU: Thank you.

(Applause)

Unit 6 Melissa Marshall: Talk nerdy to me

Part 1

Five years ago, I experienced a bit of what it must have been like to be Alice in Wonderland. Penn State asked me, a communications teacher, to teach a communications class for engineering students. And I was scared. (Laughter) Really scared. Scared of these students with their big brains and their big books and their big, unfamiliar words. But as these conversations unfolded, I experienced what Alice must have when she went down that rabbit hole and saw that door to a whole new world. That's just how I felt as I had those conversations with the students. I was amazed at the ideas that they had, and I wanted others to experience this wonderland as well. And I believe the key to opening that door is great communication.

We desperately need great communication from our scientists and engineers in order to change the world. Our scientists and engineers are the ones that are tackling our grandest challenges, from energy to environment to health care, among others, and if we don't know about it and understand it, then the work isn't done, and I believe it's our responsibility as non-scientists to have these interactions. But these great conversations can't occur if our scientists and engineers don't invite us in to see their wonderland. So scientists and engineers, please, talk nerdy to us.

Part 2

I want to share a few keys on how you can do that to make sure that we can see that your science is sexy and that your engineering is engaging. First question to answer for us: so what? Tell us why your science is relevant to us. Don't just tell me that you study trabeculae, but tell me that you study trabeculae, which is the mesh-like structure of our bones because it's important to understanding and treating osteoporosis.

And when you're describing your science, beware of jargon. Jargon is a barrier to our understanding of your ideas. Sure, you can say "spatial and temporal," but why not just say "space and time," which is so much more accessible to us? And making your ideas accessible is not the same as dumbing it down. Instead, as Einstein said, make everything as simple as possible, but no simpler. You can clearly communicate your science without compromising the ideas. A few things to consider are having examples, stories, and analogies. Those are ways to engage and excite us about your content. And when presenting your work, drop the bullet points. Have you ever wondered why they're called bullet points? (Laughter) What do bullets do? Bullets kill, and they will kill your presentation. A slide like this is not only boring, but it relies too much on the language area of our brain, and causes us to become overwhelmed. Instead, this example slide by Genevieve Brown is much more effective. It's showing that the special structure of trabeculae are so strong that they actually inspired the unique design of the Eiffel Tower. And the trick here is to use a single, readable sentence that the audience can key into if they get a bit lost, and then provide visuals which appeal to our other senses and create a deeper sense of understanding of what's being described.

Part 3

So I think these are just a few keys that can help the rest of us to open that door and see the wonderland that is science and engineering. And because the engineers that I've worked with have taught me to become really in touch with my inner nerd, I want to summarize with an equation. (Laughter) Take your science, subtract your bullet points and your jargon, divide by relevance, meaning share what's relevant to the audience, and multiply it by the passion that you have for this incredible work that you're doing, and that is going to equal incredible interactions that are full of understanding. And so, scientists and engineers, when you've solved this equation, by all means, talk nerdy to me. (Laughter) Thank you. (Applause)

Unit 7 Pico Iyer: Where is home?

Part 1

Where do you come from? It's such a simple question, but these days, of course, simple questions bring ever more complicated answers.

People are always asking me where I come from, and they're expecting me to say India, and they're absolutely right, insofar as 100 percent of my blood and ancestry does come from India. Except, I've never lived one day of my life there. I can't speak even one word of its more than 22,000 dialects. So I don't think I've really earned the right to call myself an Indian. And if "Where do you come from?" means "Where were you born and raised and educated?" then I'm entirely of that funny little country known as England, except I left England as soon as I completed my undergraduate education, and all the time I was growing up, I was the only kid in all my classes who didn't begin to look like the classic English heroes represented in our textbooks. And if "Where do you come from?" means "Where do you pay your taxes? Where do you see your doctor and your dentist?" then I'm very much of the United States, and I have been for 48 years now, since I was a really small child. Except, for many of those years, I've had to carry around this funny little pink card with green lines running through my face identifying me as a permanent alien. I do actually feel more alien the longer I live there.

(Laughter)

And if "Where do you come from?" means "Which place goes deepest inside you and where do you try to spend most of your time?" then I'm Japanese, because I've been living as much as I can for the last 25 years in Japan. Except, all of those years I've been there on a tourist visa, and I'm fairly sure not many Japanese would want to consider me one of them.

Part 2

[. . .] And for more and more of us, home has really less to do with a piece of soil than, you could say, with a piece of soul. If somebody suddenly asks me, "Where's your home?" I think about my sweetheart or my closest friends or the songs that travel with me wherever I happen to be.

[. . .] The number of people living in countries not their own now comes to 220 million, and that's an almost unimaginable number, but it means that if you took the whole population of Canada and the whole population of Australia and then the whole population of Australia again and the whole population of Canada again and doubled that number, you would still have fewer people than belong to this great floating tribe. And the number of us who live outside the old nation-state categories is increasing so quickly, by 64 million just in the last 12 years, that soon there will be more of us than there are Americans. Already, we represent the fifth-largest nation on Earth. And in fact, in Canada's largest city, Toronto, the average resident today is what used to be called a foreigner, somebody born in a very different country.

Part 3

[. . .] Many of the people living in countries not their own are refugees who never wanted to leave home and ache to go back home. But for the fortunate among us, I think the age of movement brings exhilarating new possibilities. Certainly when I'm traveling, especially to the major cities of the world, the typical person I meet today will be, let's say, a half-Korean, half-German young woman living in Paris. And as soon as she meets a half-Thai, half-Canadian young guy from Edinburgh, she recognizes him as kin. She realizes that she probably has much more in common with him than with anybody entirely of Korea or entirely of Germany. So they become friends. They fall in love. They move to New York City. (Laughter) Or Edinburgh. And the little girl who arises out of their union will of course be not Korean or German or French or Thai or Scotch or Canadian or even American, but a wonderful and constantly evolving mix of all those places. And potentially, everything about the way that young woman dreams about the world, writes about the world, thinks about the world, could be something different, because it comes out of this almost unprecedented blend of cultures. Where you come from now is much less important than where you're going. More and more of us are rooted in the future or the present tense as much as in the past. And home, we know, is not just the place where you happen to be born. It's the place where you become yourself.

Unit 8 Sanjay Dastoor: A skateboard, with a boost

Part 1

Today I'm going to show you an electric vehicle that weighs less than a bicycle, that you can carry with you anywhere, that you can charge off a normal wall outlet in 15 minutes, and you can run it for 1,000 kilometers on about a dollar of electricity. But when I say the word electric vehicle, people think about vehicles. They think about cars and motorcycles and bicycles, and the vehicles that you use every day. But if you come about it from a different perspective, you can create some more interesting, more novel concepts.

So we built something. I've got some of the pieces in my pocket here. So this is the motor. This motor has enough power to take you up the hills of San Francisco at about 20 miles per hour, about 30 kilometers an hour, and this battery, this battery right here has about six miles of range, or 10 kilometers, which is enough to cover about half of the car trips in the U.S. alone. But the best part about these components is that we bought them at a toy store. These are from remote control airplanes. And the performance of these things has gotten so good that if you think about vehicles a little bit differently, you can really change things.

So today we're going to show you one example of how you can use this. Pay attention to not only how fun this thing is, but also how the portability that comes with this can totally change the way you interact with a city like San Francisco.

Part 2

(Music) [6 Mile Range] [Top Speed Near 20mph] [Uphill Climbing] [Regenerative Braking]

(Applause) (Cheers)

So we'll show you what this thing can do. It's really maneuverable. You have a hand-held remote, so you can pretty easily control acceleration, braking, go in reverse if you'd like, also have braking. It's incredible just how light this thing is. I mean, this is something you can pick up and carry with you anywhere you go.

So I'll leave you with one of the most compelling facts about this technology and these kinds of vehicles. This uses 20 times less energy for every mile or kilometer that you travel than a car, which means not only is this thing fast to charge and really cheap to build, but it also reduces the footprint of your energy use in terms of your transportation. So instead of looking at large amounts of energy needed for each person in this room to get around in a city, now you can look at much smaller amounts and more sustainable transportation.

So next time you think about a vehicle, I hope, like us, you're thinking about something new.

Thank you.

(Applause)

Unit 9 Anne Curzan: What makes a word "real"?

Part 1

[. . .] A couple of weeks ago, I was at a dinner party and the man to my right started telling me about all the ways that the Internet is degrading the English language. He brought up Facebook, and he said, "To defriend? I mean, is that even a real word?"

I want to pause on that question: What makes a word real? My dinner companion and I both know what the verb "defriend" means, so when does a new word like "defriend" become real? Who has the authority to make those kinds of official decisions about words, anyway? Those are the questions I want to talk about today.

I think most people, when they say a word isn't real, what they mean is, it doesn't appear in a standard dictionary. That, of course, raises a host of other questions, including, who writes dictionaries?

[. . .] Even the most critical people out there tend not to be very critical about dictionaries, not distinguishing among them and not asking a whole lot of questions about who edited them. Just think about the phrase "Look it up in the dictionary," which suggests that all dictionaries are exactly the same.

Part 2

[. . .] Here's the thing: If you ask dictionary editors, what they'll tell you is they're just trying to keep up with us as we change the language. They're watching what we say and what we write and trying to figure out what's going to stick and what's not going to stick. They have to gamble, because they want to appear cutting edge and catch the words that are going to make it, such as LOL, but they don't want to appear faddish and include the words that aren't going to make it, and I think a word that they're watching right now is YOLO, you only live once.

Now I get to hang out with dictionary editors, and you might be surprised by one of the places where we hang out. Every January, we go to the American Dialect Society annual meeting, where among other things, we vote on the word of the year.

[. . .] Now, a few weeks before our vote, Lake Superior State University issues its list of banished words for the year. What is striking about this is that there's actually often quite a lot of overlap between their list and the list that we are considering for words of the year, and this is because we're noticing the same thing. We're noticing words that are coming into prominence. It's really a question of attitude. Are you bothered by language fads and language change, or do you find it fun, interesting, something worthy of study as part of a living language?

Part 3

[. . .] In retrospect, we think it's fascinating that the word "nice" used to mean silly, and that the word "decimate" used to mean to kill one in every 10. (Laughter) We think that Ben Franklin was being silly to worry about "notice" as a verb. Well, you know what? We're going to look pretty silly in a hundred years for worrying about "impact" as a verb and "invite" as a noun. The language is not going to change so fast that we can't keep up. Language just doesn't work that way. I hope that what you can do is find language change not worrisome but fun and fascinating, just the way dictionary editors do. I hope you can enjoy being part of the creativity that is continually remaking our language and keeping it robust.

So how does a word get into a dictionary? It gets in because we use it and we keep using it, and dictionary editors are paying attention to us. If you're thinking, "But that lets all of us decide what words mean," I would say, "Yes it does, and it always has." Dictionaries are a wonderful guide and resource, but there is no objective dictionary authority out there that is the final arbiter about what words mean. If a community of speakers is using a word and knows what it means, it's real. That word might be slangy, that word might be informal, that word might be a word that you think is illogical or unnecessary, but that word that we're using, that word is real.

Thank you.

(Applause)

Unit 10 Rana el Kaliouby: This app knows how you feel

Part 1

Our emotions influence every aspect of our lives, from our health and how we learn, to how we do business and make decisions, big ones and small. Our emotions also influence how we connect with one another. We've evolved to live in a world like this, but instead, we're living more and more of our lives like this—this is the text message from my daughter last night—in a world that's devoid of emotion. So I'm on a mission to change that. I want to bring emotions back into our digital experiences.

I started on this path 15 years ago. I was a computer scientist in Egypt, and I had just gotten accepted to a Ph.D. program at Cambridge University.

[. . .] At Cambridge, thousands of miles away from home, I realized I was spending more hours with my laptop than I did with any other human. Yet despite this intimacy, my laptop had absolutely no idea how I was feeling. It had no idea if I was happy, having a bad day, or stressed, confused, and so that got frustrating. Even worse, as I communicated online with my family back home, I felt that all my emotions disappeared in cyberspace. I was homesick, I was lonely, and on some days I was actually crying, but all I had to communicate these emotions was this. (Laughter) Today's technology has lots of I.Q., but no E.Q.; lots of cognitive intelligence, but no emotional intelligence.

So that got me thinking, what if our technology could sense our emotions? What if our devices could sense how we felt and reacted accordingly, just the way an emotionally intelligent friend would? Those questions led me and my team to create technologies that can read and respond to our emotions, and our starting point was the human face.

Part 2

[. . .] So the best way to demonstrate how this technology works is to try a live demo, so I need a volunteer, preferably somebody with a face. (Laughter) Cloe's going to be our volunteer today.

[. . .] As you can see, the algorithm has essentially found Cloe's face, so it's this white bounding box, and it's tracking the main feature points on her face, so her eyebrows, her eyes, her mouth, and her nose. The question is, can it recognize her expression? So we're going to test the machine. So first of all, give me your poker face. Yep, awesome. (Laughter) And then as she smiles, this is a genuine smile, it's great. So you can see the green bar go up as she smiles. Now that was a big smile. Can you try like a subtle smile to see if the computer can recognize? It does recognize subtle smiles as well. We've worked really hard to make that happen. And then eyebrow raised, indicator of surprise. Brow furrow, which is an indicator of confusion. Frown. Yes, perfect. So these are all the different action units. There's many more of them. This is just a slimmed-down demo. But we call each reading an emotion data point [. . .]

Part 3

[. . .] So, so far, we have amassed 12 billion of these emotion data points. It's the largest emotion database in the world. We've collected it from 2.9 million face videos, people who have agreed to share their emotions with us, and from 75 countries around the world. It's growing every day. It blows my mind away that we can now quantify something as personal as our emotions, and we can do it at this scale.

So what have we learned to date? Gender. Our data confirms something that you might suspect. Women are more expressive than men. Not only do they smile more, their smiles last longer, and we can now really quantify what is it that men and women respond to differently. Let's do culture: So in the United States, women are 40 percent more expressive than men, but curiously, we don't see any difference in the U.K. between men and women. (Laughter) Age: People who are 50 years and older are 25 percent more emotive than younger people. Women in their 20s smile a lot more than men the same age, perhaps a necessity for dating. But perhaps what surprised us the most about this data is that we happen to be expressive all the time [. . .]

Part 4

[. . .] Where is this data used today? In understanding how we engage with media, so understanding virality and voting behavior; and also empowering or emotion-enabling technology, and I want to share some examples that are especially close to my heart. Emotion-enabled wearable glasses can help individuals who are visually impaired read the faces of others, and it can help individuals on the autism spectrum interpret emotion, something that they really struggle with. In education, imagine if your learning apps sense that you're confused and slowed down, or that you're bored, so it's sped up, just like a great teacher would in a classroom. What if your wristwatch tracked your mood, or your car sensed that you're tired, or perhaps your fridge knows that you're stressed, so it auto-locks to prevent you from binge eating. (Laughter) I would like that, yeah. What if, when I was in Cambridge, I had access to my real-time emotion stream, and I could share that with my family back home in a very natural way, just like I would've if we were all in the same room together?

I think five years down the line, all our devices are going to have an emotion chip, and we won't remember what it was like when we couldn't just frown at our device and our device would say, "Hmm, you didn't like that, did you?"

[. . .] So as more and more of our lives become digital, we are fighting a losing battle trying to curb our usage of devices in order to reclaim our emotions. So what I'm trying to do instead is to bring emotions into our technology and make our technologies more responsive. So I want those devices that have separated us to bring us back together. And by humanizing technology, we have this golden opportunity to reimagine how we connect with machines, and therefore, how we, as human beings, connect with one another.

Thank you.

Unit 11 Richard Branson: Life at 30,000 feet

Part 1

[. . .] Chris Anderson: So, we're going to put up some slides of some of your companies here. You've started one or two in your time. So, you know, Virgin Atlantic, Virgin Records—I guess it all started with a magazine called *Student*. And then, yes, all these other ones as well. I mean, how do you do this?

Richard Branson: I read all these sort of TED instructions: you must not talk about your own business, and this, and now you ask me. So I suppose you're not going to be able to kick me off the stage, since you asked the question. (Laughter)

CA: It depends what the answer is though.

RB: No, I mean, I think I learned early on that if you can run one company, you can really run any companies. I mean, companies are all about finding the right people, inspiring those people, you know, drawing out the best in people. And I just love learning and I'm incredibly inquisitive and I love taking on, you know, the status quo and trying to turn it upside down. So I've seen life as one long learning process. And if I see—you know, if I fly on somebody else's airline and find the experience is not a pleasant one, which it wasn't, 21 years ago, then I'd think, well, you know, maybe I can create the kind of airline that I'd like to fly on. And so, you know, so got one secondhand 747 from Boeing and gave it a go.

Part 2

[. . .] CA: Didn't—weren't you just terrible at school?

RB: I was dyslexic. I had no understanding of schoolwork whatsoever. I certainly would have failed IQ tests. And it was one of the reasons I left school when I was 15 years old. And if I—if I'm not interested in something, I don't grasp it. As somebody who's dyslexic, you also have some quite bizarre situations. I mean, for instance, I've had to—you know, I've been running the largest group of private companies in Europe, but haven't been able to know the difference between net and gross. And so the board meetings have been fascinating. (Laughter) And so, it's like, good news or bad news? And generally, the people would say, oh, well that's bad news.

CA: But just to clarify, the 25 billion dollars is gross, right? That's gross? (Laughter)

RB: Well, I hope it's net actually, having—(Laughter)—I've got it right.

CA: No, trust me, it's gross. (Laughter)

RB: So, when I turned 50, somebody took me outside the boardroom and said, "Look Richard, here's a—let me draw on a diagram. Here's a net in the sea, and the fish have been pulled from the sea into this net. And that's the profits you've got left over in this little net, everything else is eaten." And I finally worked it all out.

Part 3

[. . .] CA: So seriously, is there a dark side? A lot of people would say there's no way that someone could put together this incredible collection of businesses without knifing a few people in the back, you know, doing some ugly things. You've been accused of being ruthless. There was a nasty biography written about you by someone. Is any of it true? Is there an element of truth in it?

RB: I don't actually think that the stereotype of a

businessperson treading all over people to get to the top, generally speaking, works. I think if you treat people well, people will come back and come back for more. And I think all you have in life is your reputation and it's a very small world. And I actually think that the best way of becoming a successful business leader is dealing with people fairly and well, and I like to think that's how we run Virgin.

Unit 12 Arianna Huffington: How to succeed? Get more sleep

Part 1

My big idea is a very, very small idea that can unlock billions of big ideas that are at the moment dormant inside us. And my little idea that will do that is sleep.

This is a room of Type-A women. This is a room of sleep-deprived women. And I learned the hard way, the value of sleep. Two-and-a-half years ago, I fainted from exhaustion. I hit my head on my desk. I broke my cheekbone, I got five stitches on my right eye. And I began the journey of rediscovering the value of sleep. And in the course of that, I studied, I met with medical doctors, scientists, and I'm here to tell you that the way to a more productive, more inspired, more joyful life is getting enough sleep.

And we women are going to lead the way in this new revolution, this new feminist issue.

Part 2

[. . .] I was recently having dinner with a guy who bragged that he had only gotten four hours sleep the night before. And I felt like saying to him—but I didn't say it—I felt like saying, "You know what? If you had gotten five, this dinner would have been a lot more interesting." There is now a kind of sleep deprivation one-upmanship. Especially here in Washington, if you try to make a breakfast date, and you say, "How about eight o'clock?" they're likely to tell you, "Eight o'clock is too late for me, but that's okay, I can get a game of tennis in and do a few conference calls and meet you at eight." And they think that means that they are so incredibly busy and productive, but the truth is they're not, because we, at the moment, have had brilliant leaders in business, in finance, in politics, making terrible decisions. So a high I.Q. does not mean that you're a good leader, because the essence of leadership is being able to see the iceberg before it hits the Titanic. And we've had far too many icebergs hitting our Titanics.

In fact, I have a feeling that if Lehman Brothers was Lehman Brothers and Sisters, they might still be around. (Applause) While all the brothers were busy just being hyper-connected 24/7, maybe a sister would have noticed the iceberg, because she would have woken up from a seven-and-a-half- or eight-hour sleep and have been able to see the big picture.

So as we are facing all the multiple crises in our world at the moment, what is good for us on a personal level, what's going to bring more joy, gratitude, effectiveness in our lives and be the best for our own careers is also what is best for the world. So I urge you to shut your eyes and discover the great ideas that lie inside us, to shut your engines and discover the power of sleep.

Thank you.

(Applause)

Grammar Summary

UNIT 1: Present and past tenses

Simple present
I teach children to draw.
She volunteers once a month.
He watches the news on TV every evening.

I don't like to waste food.
You don't often take care of the children.
She doesn't work on Sundays.
They don't help out much.

Do you donate to charity?
Do you recycle waste?
Does he know any volunteers?
Does this charity have branches overseas?

Where do the volunteers go after the event?
Who helps out at the organization?

How often do you volunteer?
How do they reduce the amount of trash?

Present progressive
I'm waiting for a bus.
You're listening to a podcast about global warming.

I'm not working on any projects currently.
He isn't volunteering this month.

Are we helping to reduce waste?
Is she donating her old furniture?

Simple past
She lived in Los Angeles when she was in college.
They started a new company a couple of months ago.

I worked in Seoul last year.
I learned a lot about ways to reduce pollution at the workshop last week.

I didn't know so much food was wasted.
Did you see the presentation on solar energy?

We use the simple present to talk about:

- things that are always or generally true
  I'm a nurse. I take care of sick people.
- repeated actions and routines
  I take my children to school and then go to the hospital.
- permanent situations
  She works as a doctor in a large hospital.

To form negative sentences and questions in the simple present, we use *do/don't/does/doesn't* with the main verb.

Wh- questions start with a question word (*What, Where, Who, When, Why, How*, etc.).

We use the present progressive to describe:

- events that are happening now or around now
  John is waiting for you in the lobby.
- temporary situations
  We're staying with a friend while we're visiting the city.
- trends
  The amount of trash is increasing every year.

- We use the simple past to talk about completed actions and events in the past. We often include a time phrase (*yesterday, last year*, etc.).
- To form negative sentences and questions in the simple past, we use *did/didn't* + the main verb.

Past progressive

The doctor was examining the patient.
We were studying ways to help the environment.

He wasn't working last weekend.
They weren't studying when I arrived.

Were you helping out this morning?
Were they volunteering last Sunday?

We use the past progressive to:

- talk about something that continued before and after another action
  I was watching TV when she called.

- show that something continued for some time
  I was living in Los Angeles.

- talk about past trends
  The number of volunteers was increasing.

Present perfect

Cell phones have changed how we keep in touch.
He has spent the past two days collecting trash for recycling.

They haven't met the other volunteers yet.
She hasn't worked for a charity before.

Have you ever done any volunteer work?
Has he received the letter we sent?

We use the present perfect to:

- talk about experiences or things that happened at an unspecified time in the past
  He has been to many countries.

- show that something is important in the present
  The Internet has made a huge difference in how we get information.

- show that something continues up to the present
  They have lived in Tokyo for nine years.

UNIT 2: *Will* and *going to*

Robots will become very popular.
Virtual reality will be the next big thing.

There won't be many people without a smartphone in ten years.
We probably won't ever use teleportation to travel.

Will there be people living on Mars by 2030?
Will the Internet of Things really benefit us?

I'm certain she is going to be world-famous.
We are all going to use technology more.

Machines are never going to be as creative as us.
I'm sure humans are not going to find aliens.

Are robot police going to become common?
Is the Internet of Things going to change the way we use our devices?

- We use *will* to make predictions about the future that we are certain about.
  I'm sure machines will replace people in most jobs.

- We form negative sentences with *won't* (= will not).
  There won't be many people without access to the Internet in a few years.

- We can also use *going to* to make predictions about the future. The meaning in most cases is the same as using *will* or *won't*.
  Connected devices are going to be everywhere in a few years.

UNIT 3: Cause and effect

Introduce an effect
Diabetes is a preventable disease, so it's important to have a healthy lifestyle to avoid it.

Introduce a cause
A lot of people use health and fitness wearables because they want to monitor their activity.
Many governments are spending more on health care due to aging populations.
You should exercise for at least 150 minutes a week as it has multiple health benefits.
As a result of early treatment, the patient made a full recovery.
Because of improvements in medical technology, cancer survival rates have increased.

We use the words *so*, *because*, *due to*, *as*, *as a result of*, and *because of* to link two parts of a sentence. All these words except *so* introduce a cause.

Other common linking words are *owing to* and *since*. They both introduce a cause.

- *Owing to* has a similar meaning to *due to*, *as a result of*, and *because of*.
  Owing to the heavy traffic, the doctor was late.

- *Since* has a similar meaning to *because*.
  He was told by his doctor to cut down on red meat, since too much of it can lead to heart disease.

UNIT 4: Making comparisons

Smartphones are easier to use than computers.
The headset was better than we expected.
It's a cheaper product than the one we saw in the other store.

Modern computers are much faster than ones from ten years ago.

This was the most popular app last month.

The new TV we bought is as big as our old one.

This website is not as well-designed as ours.

She has the same smartphone as me.

The way we use technology today is very different from how we used it 15 years ago.

This tablet is the least expensive, but it's also less user-friendly than the other ones.
The design of this smartphone looks the least attractive to me.

- We use the comparative form to compare two things.
- We can add the intensifier *much* to strengthen the comparison.
- We use the superlative form to compare three or more things.
- We use *as* + adjective + *as* to compare two things and say they are the same or equal.
- We use *not as* + adjective + *as* to compare two things and say that one is less than the other.
- We also use *the same … as* and *different from / than* to compare things.
- We can also use *less … than* and *the least* with an adjective.

Regular adjectives

Adjective	Comparative	Superlative
cheap	cheaper	the cheapest
big	bigger	the biggest
simple	simpler	the simplest
healthy	healthier	the healthiest
expensive	more expensive	the most expensive
important	more important	the most important

Irregular adjectives

Adjective	Comparative	Superlative
good	better	the best
bad	worse	the worst
many	more	the most
little	less	the least

UNIT 5: The passive

The river was cleaned up last year.
The river wasn't cleaned up last year.

New facilities were built for the local residents.
New facilities weren't built for the local residents.

The lives of many people were improved by social entrepreneurs.
Students from rural areas were recruited by the college.

Was the project stopped due to lack of money?

Were the houses painted by the villagers?

- We use the passive when we want to focus on an action or the object of the action, rather than on the person who is doing the action.

- We often use the passive because we don't know who or what did the action, or when it isn't important to know. If we want to say who does or did the action (the agent), we use the passive verb + *by* agent.

- We form the simple past passive with the simple past of the verb *be* (*was/were*) + past participle.

We use the simple past passive:

- to talk about past facts
  Barefoot College was founded by Sanjit Roy.

- to describe a past process or series of events
  The corporation was set up, plans were developed, and a new transport system was constructed.

UNIT 6: Verb patterns with *-ing* and infinitive

He dislikes receiving calls late at night.
The presenter recommended not using social media so much.

They decided to create a new social media company.
I intend to send a card to congratulate him on getting engaged.

She hates to lose / hates losing.
He prefers to communicate / prefers communicating by email.

- We use the verb + *-ing* pattern with some verbs, which are never followed by the infinitive. The negative form of this pattern is *not* + *-ing*.
  She usually avoids texting her boss.
  I regret not writing to them.

- We use verb + infinitive with some verbs, which are never followed by *-ing*.
  We agreed to keep in touch via email.

- Some verbs can follow either pattern without changing the basic meaning.
  I love to check / love checking my social media accounts.

She stopped to call her friend. (= She stopped what she was doing and called her friend.)
She stopped chatting with her friend. (= She was chatting with her friend and then she stopped.)

He remembered to go see his sister yesterday. (= This was an action that he needed to do.)

They remembered going on their first vacation together. (= This was a past experience that they remembered.)

The Internet allows us all to keep in touch easily.
He taught his grandmother how to take videos.
Should we invite Jing to take part in the webinar?

- Some verbs can follow either pattern, but there is a change in meaning of the sentence.
  I forgot to buy the books for her. (= I didn't buy the books for her because I forgot.)
  I won't forget buying my first smartphone.
  (= I bought a smartphone and the experience is something that I will not forget.)

- We use verb + object + infinitive with some verbs.
  She persuaded me to sign up for a new social media account.

verb + -ing	verb + infinitive	verb + -ing / verb + infinitive with similar meanings	verb + object + infinitive
avoid	agree	begin	allow
consider	aim	continue	ask
dislike	arrange	hate	encourage
enjoy	choose	like	expect
finish	decide	love	force
imagine	expect	prefer	help
keep	hope	start	like
mind	intend		invite
practice	learn	**verb + -ing / verb + infinitive with different meanings**	need
recommend	manage		persuade
regret	need		remind
risk	plan	forget	teach
suggest	prepare	remember	tell
	promise	stop	want
	want		would

UNIT 7: Present perfect progressive

I have been traveling around the world.
She has been learning about migration patterns this semester.

We have been researching this topic for the last few months.
My sister has been staying at a resort since Monday.

The populations of many countries haven't been increasing for several years.
He hasn't been living in the United States for the past ten years.

Have you been doing a lot of overtime recently?
Has she been working on her project today?

I have known her for many years.
He has liked performing on stage since he was a child.

- We form the present perfect progressive with *have/has + been + -ing*.
- We use *for* to introduce the duration of an event or action and *since* to say when the event/action began.

We use the present perfect progressive to talk about:

- the duration of an action that started in the past and is continuing now
  They have been arguing about this for three hours / since 2 p.m.

- how someone has spent their time recently
  My friends have been chatting all evening.

- Stative verbs are used to express a state, rather than an action. We don't use these verbs with the progressive form.
  She has always believed that migrants contribute greatly to society.

Stative verbs

| believe | hate | like |
| belong | know | recognize |

UNIT 8: Predictions with *will* and *might*

Predictions with *will*
I think transportation will be faster and more efficient in the future.
I don't think many people will buy a ticket to go into space.

There won't be many people who can afford to take a space vacation.
Electric cars won't be as popular as regular cars for quite a few years.

Will people ever be able to use teleportation to travel?
Will there be driverless cars in the next two or three years?

Predictions with *might*
People might be able to travel around the world in 24 hours within a few years.
I might not need the car today.

- We use *will* to make predictions about the future that we are certain about.
  New types of transportation will change how we travel.

- We often use *will* with *I think / I hope / I expect / I'm sure / I don't think*.
  I'm sure the price of oil will rise over the next few years.

- We often add qualifiers like *certainly*, *definitely*, or *probably*.
  Space travel will definitely not be cheap.

- We use *might* to talk about events in the future that we think are possible, but we are not certain about.
  Electric vehicles might be more popular than regular vehicles in 15 years.

UNIT 9: *Used to*

I used to write letters to my friends.
He used to look up words he didn't know in the dictionary.

Cell phones didn't use to be small and light.
English didn't use to be a global language.

When did people use to use the word *groovy*?
Did your teacher use to encourage you to keep a journal?

- We use *used to* to talk about habits or states that took place in the past but do not happen or exist now.
  I used to work as a dictionary editor, but now I write novels.

- We can also use *would* to talk about the past. In such cases, it has a similar meaning to *used to*.
  When I was studying Spanish, I would write down a few new words to learn every day.

UNIT 10: Reported speech

Kate: "I'm doing a report on emotional intelligence."
Kate said (that) she is / was doing a report on emotional intelligence.

Mary: "I took an EQ test last year."
Mary said (that) she took / had taken an EQ test last year.

Josh: "Scientists are developing robots that judge emotions."
Josh said (that) scientists were developing robots that judge emotions.

Bill: "As part of their research, they were studying facial expressions."
Bill said (that) as part of their research, they were / had been studying facial expressions.

Jin: "Emotion-sensing technology will probably become popular within ten years."
Jin said (that) emotion-sensing technology would probably become popular within ten years.

Miki: "Jon, have you ever taken an IQ test?"
Miki asked Jon if / whether he had ever taken an IQ test.

Sunhee: "What kind of issues will facial recognition technology raise?"
Sunhee asked what kind of issues facial recognition technology would raise.

He admitted that IQ was not always a good measure of success.

The presenter told the audience to think about the last time they got annoyed.

She told him that learning a new language would help improve his memory.

He suggested researching the privacy challenges emotionally intelligent technology could create.

They promised to get in touch soon after the job interview.

According to Daniel Goleman, EQ is just as important as IQ.

- We use reported speech to report someone's words or thoughts.
- The most common reporting verb for statements is *say*. After the reporting verb, *that* is optional.

Verb tenses often change when we report what someone said.

- Simple present becomes simple past.
- Simple past usually becomes past perfect, though it may stay as simple past.
- Present progressive becomes past progressive.
- Past progressive becomes past perfect progressive.
- The modal verbs *might*, *should*, *would*, and *could* don't usually change. *Will* becomes *would*. *Must* becomes *had to*.
- The most common reporting verb for questions is *ask*.
- We use *if* or *whether* to report yes/no questions.
- We use the same *wh-* word to report questions with *who*, *where*, *what*, *why*, etc.

Some reporting verbs use other patterns:

- verb + *that*
  Verbs that use this pattern include *admit*, *agree*, *deny*, *explain*, *realize*, *say*, and *warn*.

- verb + object + *(not)* + infinitive
  Verbs that use this pattern include *advise*, *ask*, *convince*, *encourage*, *invite*, *persuade*, *remind*, *tell*, and *warn*.

- verb + object + *that*
  Verbs that use this pattern include *advise*, *persuade*, *tell*, and *warn*.

- verb + *-ing*
  Verbs that use this pattern include *admit*, *advise*, *deny*, *mention*, *propose*, *recommend*, and *suggest*.

- verb + *(not)* + infinitive
  Verbs that use this pattern include *agree*, *offer*, *promise*, *refuse*, and *threaten*.

- *according to*
  We use *according to* when we want to report a fact as described by somebody.

Pronoun, adjective, and adverb changes

Direct speech	Reported speech	Direct speech	Reported speech
I	he/she	now	then
we	they	today	that day
my	his/her	tomorrow	the next day
our	their	yesterday	the previous day
here	there	last night	the night before
this classroom	that classroom		

UNIT 11: Modals of necessity

You *must* be flexible to be a good leader.
If you want to succeed, you *mustn't* give up.

Companies *have to* accept that failure is often a necessary part of business.
You *don't have to* have a degree to start your own business.

You *need to* take risks sometimes to grow your business.
People *don't need to* be ruthless to get to the top.

Businesses *should* aim to give customers something exciting and new.
Leaders *shouldn't* forget that employee job satisfaction is very important for success.

- We use *must*, *have to*, and *need to* to say that something is necessary. We often use *must* and *have to* to talk about rules.
- We use *mustn't* to talk about things that are not permitted, when there is an obligation not to do them.
- We use *don't have to* and *don't need to* to say something is not necessary, or there is no obligation to do something.
- We use *should* and *shouldn't* to give advice or to make a recommendation about what is the right or wrong thing to do.

UNIT 12: Second conditional

If workdays *were* shorter, I *would have* more time to relax.

If I *had* more time, I *would go* to the gym.

If I *could do* any job, I *would be* a dance instructor.

If she *lived* by the sea, she *would go* for a swim every day.

Eating more fruits and vegetables *would* help.

- We form the second conditional using: *If* + simple past, *would* + infinitive (without *to*)

if-clause	main clause
If + simple past	*would* + infinitive (without *to*)

- We can use *if* in two positions: *if*-clause first or main clause first. When the *if*-clause is at the beginning of the sentence, we use a comma to separate it from the main clause.
  If I ate less fast food, I would lose weight.
  I would lose weight if I ate less fast food.

We use the second conditional to:

- talk about situations that are imaginary or not probable
  If I had my own gym, I would use it every day.

- give advice (with *were*)
  If I were you, I would exercise more.

- talk about hypothetical outcomes with no *if*-clause
  Getting more sleep would be good.

Acknowledgements

The Author and Publisher would like to thank the following teaching professionals for their valuable input during the development of this series:

Coleeta Paradise Abdullah, Certified Training Center; **Tara Amelia Arntsen**, Northern State University; **Estela Campos**; **Federica Castro**, Pontificia Universidad Católica Madre y Maestra; **Amy Cook**, Bowling Green State University; **Carrie Cheng**, School of Continuing and Professional Studies, the University of Hong Kong; **Mei-ho Chiu**, Soochow University; **Anthony Sean D'Amico**, SDH Institute; **Wilder Yesid Escobar Almeciga**, Universidad El Bosque; **Rosa E. Vasquez Fernandez**, English for International Communication; **Touria Ghaffari**, The Beekman School; **Rosario Giraldez**, Alianza Cultural Uruguay Estados Unidos; **William Haselton**, NC State University; **Yu Huichun**, Macau University of Science and Technology; **Michelle Kim**, TOPIA Education; **Jay Klaphake**, Kyoto University of Foreign Studies; **Kazuteru Kuramoto**, Keio Senior High School; **Michael McCollister**, Feng Chia University; **Jennifer Meldrum**, EC English Language Centers; **Holly Milkowart**, Johnson County Community College; **Nicholas Millward**, Australian Centre for Education; **Stella Maris Palavecino**, Buenos Aires English House; **Youngsun Park**, YBM; **Adam Parmentier**, Mingdao High School; **Jennie Popp**, Universidad Andrés Bello; **Terri Rapoport**, ELS Educational Services; **Erich Rose**, Auburn University; **Yoko Sakurai**, Aichi University; **Mark D. Sheehan**, Hannan University; **DongJin Shin**, Hankuk University of Foreign Studies; **Shizuka Tabara**, Kobe University; **Jeffrey Taschner**, AUA Language Center; **Hadrien Tournier**, Berlitz Corporation; **Rosa Vasquez**, JFK Institute; **Jindarat De Vleeschauwer**, Chiang Mai University; **Tamami Wada**, Chubu University; **Colin Walker**, Myongii University; **Elizabeth Yoon**, Hanyang University; **Keiko Yoshida**, Konan University

And special thanks to: **Peter Draw, Tara Hirebet, Kate Chong, Carrie Cousins, Martín Andrade, Neil Anderson, Janice Reis Lodge, Charles Browne, Craig Albrightson, Priscilla Shunmugam, Mary Kadera**

Credits

Photo Credits

Cover Gerd Ludwig/National Geographic Creative, **3** Kevork Djansezian/Getty Images News/Getty Images, **4** (tl) (tr) © James Duncan Davidson/TED, (cl) © Ryan Lash/TED, (cr) (bl) (br) © James Duncan Davidson/TED, **5** (tl) (tr) © James Duncan Davidson/TED, (cl) © TED, (cr) © Marla Aufmuth/TED, (bl) © Robert Leslie/TED, (br) © Michael Brands/2010 TED Conferences, **6** (tl1) Roslan Rahman/AFP/Getty Images, (tl2) Kazuhiro Nogi/AFP/Getty Images, (cl1) Guido Mieth/Taxi/Getty Images, (cl2) AP Images/Eric Risberg, (bl1) Frances Roberts/Alamy Stock Photo (bl2) © Adelina Iliev, **8** (tl1) Gerd Ludwig/National Geographic Creative, (tl2) © Krista Rossow, (cl1) AP Images/Icon Sportswire, (cl2) Sarawut Inatrob/500px Prime, (bl1) Victor Chavez/WireImage/Getty Images, (bl2) Lynsey Addario/National Geographic Creative, **10–11** © Marla Aufmuth/TED, **12** © Michael Brands/TED, **13** © James Duncan Davidson/TED, **14** Roslan Rahman/AFP/Getty Images, **15** Courtesy of Peter Draw, **17** © Blare Gooch, **18–19** © Cathy Lee, **21** © James Duncan Davidson/TED, **22** © Gabrielle Plucknette, **24** Jonas Gratzer/LightRocket/Getty Images, **25** © James Duncan Davidson/TED, **26** Kazuhiro Nogi/AFP/Getty Images, **27** © Daylon Soh, **29** Javier Larrea/Age Footstock/Getty Images, **30–31** © YouTube, **33** © James Duncan Davidson/TED, **34** © TED, **35** © James Duncan Davidson/TED, **36** Justin Sullivan/Getty Images, **37** © Ryan Lash/TED, **38** Guido Mieth/Taxi/Getty Images, **39** © Kate Chong, **41** Aung Naing Soe/Anadolu Agency/Getty Images, **43** Stephane De Sakutin/AFP/Getty Images, **45** © Ryan Lash/TED, **46** © TED, **47** © Ryan Lash/TED, **48** Jean-Francois Monier/AFP/Getty Images, **49** © Cengage Learning, **51** © James Duncan Davidson/TED, **52** Iryna Denysova/Shutterstock.com, **53** Courtesy of Carrie Cousins, **55** Scott Eells/Bloomberg/Getty Images, **56–57** AP Images/Eric Risberg, **59** © James Duncan Davidson/TED, **60** Carl De Souza/AFP/Getty Images, **61** © James Duncan Davidson/TED, **62** David Ramos/Stringer/Getty Images News/Getty Images, **63** © James Duncan Davidson/TED, **64** Frances Roberts/Alamy Stock Photo, **65** Courtesy of Martín Andrade, **66** (l) De Agostini/Getty Images, (r) Laurie Noble/Photolibrary/Getty Images, **67** Loop Images/UIG/Getty Images, **68–69** © Dieter Telemans/Panos Pictures, **71** © James Duncan Davidson/TED, **73** Andrea Pistolesi/Photolibrary/Getty Images, **74** Lisa Maree Williams/Stringer/Getty Images News/Getty Images, **75** © James Duncan Davidson/TED, **76** © Adelina Iliev, **77** Courtesy of Neil Anderson, **79** © Jiangang Wang, **81** © Brian Yen, **83** © James Duncan Davidson/TED, **84** © Malcolm Nason, **85** © James Duncan Davidson/TED, **86** Aksonov/E+/Getty Images, **87** © Cengage Learning, **89** © James Duncan Davidson/TED, **90** Gerd Ludwig/National Geographic Creative, **91** © Cengage Learning, **93** Fakrul Jamil Photography/Moment/Getty Images, **97** © James Duncan Davidson/TED, **99** Alberto Manuel Urosa Toledanok/Moment/Getty Images, **100** epa european pressphoto agency b.v./Alamy Stock Photo, **101** © James Duncan Davidson/TED, **102** © Krista Rossow, **103** © Erik Urdahl, **105** John Gurzinski/AFP/Getty Images, **107** Kevork Djansezian/Getty Images News/Getty Images, **109** (t) © James Duncan Davidson/TED, (b) Courtesy of Wheego, **111** Courtesy of Boosted Boards, **112** © Shweeb, **113** © TED, **114** AP Images/Icon Sportswire, **115** Courtesy of Charles Browne, **117** Culture Club/Hulton Archive/Getty Images, **118–119** Alain Jocard/AFP/Getty Images, **121** © TED, **123** Raphael Gaillarde/Gamma-Rapho/Getty Images, **124** Ajayptp/Shutterstock.com, **125** © Cengage Learning, **127** © Marla Aufmuth/TED, **128** Sarawut Inatrob/500px Prime, **129** © Craig Albrightson, **131** David Woolfall/Getty Images, **132–133** © Aldebaran, **135** © Marla Aufmuth/TED, **136** © TED, **137** © Marla Aufmuth/TED, **138** Chris24/Alamy Stock Photo, **139** © Robert Leslie/TED, **140** Victor Chavez/WireImage/Getty Images, **141** Xinhua/Alamy Stock Photo, **143** NG Images/Alamy Stock Photo, **144–145** Jason Alden/Bloomberg/Getty Images, **147** © Robert Leslie/TED, **150** Dimas Ardian/Bloomberg/Getty Images, **151** © Michael Brands/2010 TED Conferences, **152** Lynsey Addario/National Geographic Creative, **153** Wunkley/Alamy Stock Photo, **155** Aaron Ontiveroz/The Denver Post/Getty Images, **157** © Peter Wurmli, **159** © Michael Brands/TED, **161** Jeff T. Green/Getty Images News/Getty Images, **162** Jeff Greenberg/UIG/Getty Images, **163** © Cengage Learning, **168** (l) leungchopan/Shutterstock.com, (r) Wayne0216/Shutterstock.com

Illustration & Infographic Credits

16, 28, 40, 54, 66, 78, 92, 104, 116, 130, 142, 154 emc design; **18, 42, 52, 80, 98, 148, 156** MPS North America LLC; **94–95** "Migration by the Numbers: The Most Diverse Cities in the World" by Josh Covarrubias, September 2, 2014; https://www.good.is/infographics/the-most-diverse-cities-in-the-world. Reprinted with permission from Good Magazine and Ford Motor Company

Data sources for infographics: **28** Bernard Marr, www.intel.com, **40** getreferralmd.com, mhealthintelligence.com, uk.reuters.com, **54** www.mycustomer.com, **66** melaka-riverwalk.blogspot.sg, www.theantdaily.com, www.wepa-db.net, **78** circle.espire.com/thread/6552, **92** International Organization for Migration, Pew Research Center, **104** www.dailymail.co.uk, www.digitaltrends.com, www.computerworld.com, www.bloomberg.com, www.skytran.com, **116** www.inquisitr.com, ideas.ted.com, www.mirror.co.uk, mentalfloss.com, blog.oxforddictionaries.com, **130** 2013 Hogan Assessment Systems, Inc., **142** www.inc.com, **154** National Sleep Foundation

Text Credits

105 Adapted from "Elon Musk's Hyperloop Idea for Sonic Tubular Travel Gets Real": news.nationalgeographic.com, February 2016